Fergal Keane

SEASON OF BLOOD
A RWANDAN JOURNEY

PENGUIN BOOKS

PENGUIN BOOKS

Published by the Penguin Group
Penguin Books Ltd, 27 Wrights Lane, London W8 5TZ, England
Penguin Books USA Inc., 375 Hudson Street, New York, New York 10014, USA
Penguin Books Australia Ltd, Ringwood, Victoria, Australia
Penguin Books Canada Ltd, 10 Alcorn Avenue, Toronto, Ontario, Canada M4V 3B2
Penguin Books (NZ) Ltd, 182–190 Wairau Road, Auckland 10, New Zealand

Penguin Books Ltd, Registered Offices: Harmondsworth, Middlesex, England

First published by Viking 1995
Published in Penguin Books 1996
3 5 7 9 10 8 6 4

The acknowledgements on pp. xi–xiii constitute an extension of this copyright page

Printed in England by Clays Ltd, St Ives plc

PENGUIN BOOKS

SEASON OF BLOOD

Fergal Keane was appointed Southern Africa Correspondent of the BBC in 1990, having covered the region since the early 1980s. He was named as Amnesty International's Human Rights Reporter of the Year in the 1994 Sony Awards. He won the Reporter of the Year Award at the New York Festival of Radio in 1994. His previous book, *The Bondage of Fear*, is also available in Penguin. *Season of Blood* was the winner of the 1995 Orwell Prize.

Fergal Keane was born in London and educated in Ireland, where he keeps a small cottage on the south-east coast.

*Dedicated to the memory of the people of
Nyarubuye parish, murdered, April 1994*

When evil-doing comes like falling rain, nobody calls out, 'stop!'
When crimes begin to pile up they become invisible.
When sufferings become unendurable the cries are no longer
  heard. The cries, too, fall like rain in summer.

— BERTOLT BRECHT

The grave is only half full. Who will help us fill it?

— RADIO MILLE COLLINES, *Rwanda*, April 1994

Contents

Acknowledgements

I found this a difficult book to write and am indebted to several people whose kindness and advice helped to make the task easier. First and foremost a thank-you to my wife, Anne, whose support and understanding was my mainstay. While the book is my own story, the Rwandan journey was, of course, a team effort. I am for ever grateful to my colleagues and travelling partners David Harrison, Glenn Middleton, Rizu Hamid and Hamilton Wende. They were good friends and total professionals. My thanks also to Chris Wyld at the BBC for suggesting that I go to Rwanda. Also to Vin Ray, Chris Cramer, Glenwyn Benson and Tim Gardam.

At the *Panorama* office in London, Lucy Crowe, Jim Baker, Faith Nyindeba and Ali Yusuf Mugenzi worked against the odds to ensure that our film on the genocide was edited and broadcast in record time. Thank you to Julia Bourhill in Johannesburg for making the all important travel arrangements.

I am also deeply grateful for the advice and information provided by African Rights, whose report on the Rwandan genocide is the most comprehensive account yet written. It provided invaluable source material on the roots of the genocide. Also to Médecins Sans Frontières, Amnesty

International and Human Rights Watch, who have produced informative and insightful reports. In Rwanda, Lt Frank Ndore, information officer of the Rwandan Patriotic Front (RPF), was open-minded and helpful, and never sought to interfere with our journalistic freedom. Major Guy Plante of the United Nations Assistance Mission in Rwanda (UNAMIR) did his utmost to provide help and information.

Mark Doyle of the BBC and Aidan Hartley of Reuters were always kind and helpful in Kigali, my thanks to them both. Among other journalists whose work proved an inspiration were Chris McGreal of the *Guardian*, Mark Huband of the *Observer*, Sam Kiley of *The Times* and Robert Bloch of the *Independent*. My friend Eric Ransdell, of *US News and World Report Magazine*, provided vital advice on the 'do's and don'ts' of reporting in Rwanda. To Tony Lacey and Donna Poppy at Viking, the usual, eternal thanks for wise advice and patience. Similar thanks to my agent Gill Coleridge, whose timely faxes ensured I finished the book.

My greatest debt, however, is to the survivors of the genocide. They gave me their time and their stories, and I am humbled by the recollection of their quiet dignity in the face of appalling suffering. I will never forget them.

Grateful acknowledgement is made for permission to reproduce extracts from the following copyright works: to

ACKNOWLEDGEMENTS

Reed Consumer Books for *Poems 1913–1956* by Bertolt Brecht, translated by John Willett, published by Methuen London; to African Rights for *Rwanda: Death, Despair and Defiance*, published by African Rights; to A. P. Watt Ltd on behalf of Michael Yeats for 'A Prayer for My Daughter' by W. B. Yeats, first published in *Poetry* in November 1919, and included in *Michael Robartes and the Dancer* in 1921.

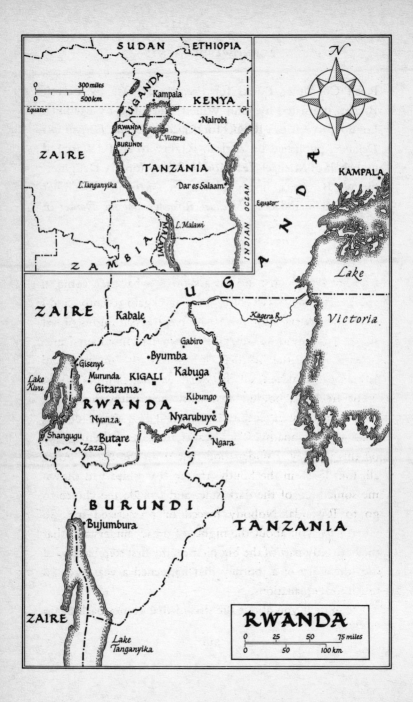

PROLOGUE

Bloodlines

I do not know what dreams ask of us, what they come to collect. But they have come again and again recently, and I have no answers. I thought that after the bad nights of last summer the dead had abandoned me, had mouldered into memory. But the brothers and sisters, the mothers and fathers and children, all the great wailing families of the night are back, holding fast with their withering hands, demanding my attention. Understand first that I do not want your sympathy. The dreams are part of the baggage on this journey. I understood that from the outset. After all, four years in the South African townships had shown me something of the dark side, and I made the choice to go to Rwanda. Nobody forced or pressurized me. So when I tell you about the nights of dread, understand that they are only part of the big picture, the first step backward into the story of a journey that happened a year ago. So much for explanations.

Let me tell you about the dream that comes back again

and again, the 'big bad one', as I have started to call it. I am asleep and become aware of hands creeping up and down my body. They prod and probe until I am awake, and in a startled moment I realize that I am lying at the bottom of a pile of rotting corpses. But they are moving, like a mound of eels at the fishmarket, or like snakes, things that slip and slither. I am being passed up through the layers of the moving dead. That is why the hands are touching me, pulling and pushing me up to the top. But I do not want to go to the top. Because up there is a man with a machete. He is looking for me. He has spent all day looking for me and is sure that I am hiding in the pile of bodies. The corpses are intent on betraying me and I am paralysed with fear. There is nothing I can do; I am helplessly pushed up through the smell of the dead towards the sunlight, where a man is waiting to kill me. I thought I had survived. I thought I had made it through, that the killers had passed me by and gone on to another village. But Christ forgive the dead, they have called the knifeman back. 'One of us still lives,' they cry. 'One of us still lives.' And now, any second now, I am going to be delivered to the top of the pile, where a man with bloody eyes and beer on his breath will sweep me away. If I am lucky the blow will cut my skull in two, massive brain damage, instant death. If not, I will linger, moaning and gasping with thirst, breathing the last rotten breaths of life until death comes as a sweet mercy. As I am about to be handed up, I wake out of the dream, bolt upright, feeling the pillow wet, my t-shirt sodden, and the darkness close and warm.

I am not the only one who is troubled at night. Many of my friends who went to Rwanda speak of dreams in which the dead visit them. I know a few who say they can detach, separate it out from their 'real lives'. I don't believe it. It touched us all in different ways. There are friends of mine who still mourn the dead of Rwanda, who cannot bare to watch the endless stream of horror stories dripping out of Central Africa. But like me they always end up watching, listening for scraps of news about the places they travelled through and the people they knew. How can I best describe it? It is a mixture of dread fascination, sorrow for what we learned and lost in the short weeks of chaos, a mind weariness that feeds itself by replaying the old tapes over and over. We reach for the off-switch but in the darkness cannot find it.

In my own case I have gone through a few different stages of escape and involvement. At first I determinedly avoided stories in the newspapers about Rwanda, changing the subject when people asked me, as so many did, 'What was it like?' Of late that has begun to change. I no longer run from the subject, although there is no way of conveying what it was really like without giving you my dreams. My journey into Rwanda was about following the lines of blood and history; about sleeping with the smell of death, fear and hatred; about exhaustion and loss and tears and in some strange ways even love. For me to make sense of that journey, however, I cannot write in terms of facts alone. So bear with me when the road runs down into the valleys of the heart and mind and soul. For this is a diary of an encounter with evil beyond any scope of reference I might have had when the journey began.

Although I had seen war before, had seen the face of cruelty, Rwanda belonged in a nightmare zone where my capacity to understand, much less rationalize, was overwhelmed. This was a country of corpses and orphans and terrible absences. This was where the spirit withered.

This book is the story of my own journey into the Rwandan genocide. During my journey in Rwanda I kept some diary notes and together with photographs and film they are my personal record of the several weeks I spent there. Much of what follows in this book is drawn from these sources, but a great deal more comes from memory. I have not found myself struggling for recall; the images and voices of that time are still terribly fresh in my mind. In writing about Rwanda, I am conscious that my words will always be unequal to the task of conveying the full horror of the crime of genocide. For what I encountered was evil in a form that frequently rendered me inarticulate. This was evil as a presence, not as a word or concept. I travelled to Rwanda in the first place to record a documentary for the BBC's *Panorama* programme. The team of four who made the journey with me were David Harrison, one of the BBC's most respected producers; Tony Wende, a sound recordist and novelist who was a friend from Johannesburg; Glenn Middleton, a cameraman who mixed rugged common sense with extraordinary sensitivity; and Rizu Hamid, a producer who grew up in Africa and whose bravery in dangerous situations was remarkable. I mention them here because they are an important part of this book. They shared the dangers and the darkness of the journey, and are part of my story and my survival. They were my saviours in different ways during and after the journey. As you come to know them in these pages I hope that their goodness comes shining through the gloom.

When the genocide started on the night of 6 April 1994, I was sitting at home in Johannesburg preparing for the multi-racial elections in South Africa. To be frank I paid only scant attention to the news reports emerging from Kigali. I have vague recollections of news bulletins describing how the aircraft carrying Juvénal Habyarimana, the president of Rwanda, and Cyprien Ntaryamira, the president of Burundi, had crashed in the grounds of the presidential palace in Kigali. In the days that followed there came a succession of stories about massacres across Rwanda. I was too preoccupied with the dramatic events unfolding in South Africa to give the matter anything more than cursory attention. Colleagues from London and Nairobi were being dispatched to Rwanda, and there didn't seem much point in my becoming sidetracked. The world's attention was focused on the elections and, having spent four years preparing for that moment, I was in no mood to head for Rwanda. In the second week of April film began to arrive in Johannesburg for transmission to British and American television networks. Much of the material seemed to be coming from the border between Rwanda and Tanzania, the Rusomo Falls Bridge, across which tens of thousands of refugees were pouring each day. There were some fearful pictures coming out of Kigali: mounds of bodies and roadblocks manned by machete-wielding gangs. The general consensus among those of us watching the pictures and those who had taken them was that Rwanda was a madhouse, a primitive torture chamber where rival tribes were busy settling ancient scores. I could not, watching the apocalyptic images unfolding on the video screens, imagine Rwanda as a country in its own right – a place with cities and schools and universities, with a wide diversity of media and political organizations, a country with musicians and poets. The idea that the madness might have been planned, that it was the direct result of political scheming, was far from my thoughts. I knew only that large-scale violence had been a feature of Rwandan life since independence. Both Rwanda and its neighbour Burundi had seen frequent massacres of one ethnic group or another. To most in the international community the words 'Tutsi' and 'Hutu' were synonymous with tribal slaughter.

The mass of early reporting of the Rwandan killings conveyed the sense that the genocide was the result of some innate inter-ethnic loathing that had erupted into irrational violence. This probably had a lot to do with the fact that major news organizations visited Rwanda and neighbouring Burundi only when there was major violence: in for a week or two to cover the slaughter and then back out again. A friend of mine, Sam Kiley of the London *Times*, rightly describes this as the 'kids in the fridge school of journalism' – in other words, a journalism driven by stories of horror but markedly lacking in analysis or historical context.

The coverage of violence in Central Africa, beginning with the horrors of the Congo in the sixties and seventies, has followed a predictable pattern. As soon as news of the killings begins to spread, the cameras arrive and the focus of attention is almost universally on the body count and the plight of the survivors. If there are Europeans to be rescued they are invariably the main news priority. The political, social and psychological factors that play a part in shaping the madness are given little analysis.

Much of the coverage of Rwanda in the early days neglected the part that power and money had played in the calculations of those who launched the genocide. Where television is concerned, African news is generally only big news when it involves lots of dead bodies. The higher the mound, the greater the possibility that the world will, however briefly, send its camera teams and correspondents. Once the story has gone 'stale', i.e. there are no new bodies and the refugees are down to a trickle, the circus moves on. The powerful images leave us momentarily horrified but largely ignorant, what somebody memorably described as having 'compassion without understanding'. Thus a well-planned campaign of politically and materially motivated slaughter can come to be explained away as an ancient tribal conflict because the men and women on the ground have been moved on before there is time to investigate properly. This is more true of television than of any other media, but several of the world's leading newspapers also bought the line, in the initial stages, that the killings were a straightforward 'tribal war'.

Rwanda's genocide was not a simple matter of mutual hatred between tribes erupting into irrational violence. Neither were the mass killings the result of a huge and sudden outpouring of rage on the part of Hutus following the murder of their president. The killings – and there is ample documentary evidence to prove this – were planned long in advance by a clique close to President Habyarimana himself. This clique – which included members of the president's immediate family and his in-laws – bitterly resented the prospect of power-sharing with the Tutsi minority. Any democratization of Rwanda's effective one-party state would have had disastrous consequences for the clique, who had powerful backers in the army and who had created their own civilian militia – the Interahamwe – to prepare for the day of vengeance against those who would seek a share of power. For several years prior to the genocide Hutus were exposed to an ongoing and virulent campaign of anti-Tutsi brainwashing. The report of the human rights group African Rights (*Death, Despair and Defiance*) provides a comprehensive and damning account

8

of this process of brainwashing and is recommended reading for anyone who doubts that the genocide was well planned.

The ostensible targets of the hatred were the rebels of the Rwandan Patriotic Front (RPF), who had launched an invasion of the country from neighbouring Uganda in October 1990. But the subtext of the numerous public condemnations of the RPF was clear enough: no Tutsi was to be trusted. All were members of a fifth column planning to reimpose a Tutsi autocracy on Rwanda. To peasants with a long folk memory of past Tutsi misrule, the warnings and the increasingly hysterical propaganda had a powerful effect. Tens of thousands became infected – and I can think of no other word that can describe the condition – by an anti-Tutsi psychosis; they were convinced through newspapers, radio and the frequent public speeches of Habyarimana's closest supporters that the Tutsis were going to turn them into beasts of the field once again.

The Hutu extremists, most of them members or supporters of the ruling party, produced a set of Ten Commandments that dictated how Hutus should treat their Tutsi neighbours. Among other things it described as 'traitors' any Hutus who married, befriended or employed Tutsis; all Tutsis were dishonest and they were to be excluded from business and from positions of influence in education; crucially the Commandments – given wide circulation in Rwanda – urged Hutus to 'stop having mercy on the Batutsi'. This last injunction was to be obeyed by thousands of Hutu peasants when the genocide began. The theology of hate espoused by the extremists was remarkably similar to that of the Nazis in their campaign against the Jews prior to the outbreak of the Second World War. It was designed to marginalize the Tutsis and create an atmosphere in which their mass destruction would be acceptable, almost inevitable.

The role of the privately owned radio station Radio Mille Collines has been widely mentioned in reporting of the Rwandan genocide. Controlled by Hutu extremists with close links to Habyarimana's family, it was also financially supported by the president. On 6 April, the day of the plane crash, Radio Mille Collines told its audience that 'Tutsis needed to be killed'. The theme was to dominate the station's broadcasts for weeks. The official state radio was only marginally less virulent, constantly calling on the Hutus to rise up and defend Rwanda against the invasion of the *inyenzi*, or 'cockroaches'. Several privately owned newspapers and journals were harnessed for the task of disseminating hate propaganda. As far as the training of the militia is concerned, there is abundant evidence implicating senior government ministers and government officials with responsibility for its genocidal agenda. Foreign diplomats, a few visiting journalists and human rights experts had been warning for several months about the training of large groups of armed Hutu extremists. Given the kind of hatred being spewed out on radio and in the newspapers, nobody could have doubted what the militia was being prepared for. The United Nations, African Rights and the new Rwandan government have prepared lists of ministers and army officers and local officials for the purpose of war crimes trials. Nearly all had been active in promoting Hutu nationalism and obsessive anti-Tutsi propaganda long before the genocide actually occurred. At its most obvious this could take the form of simple murder – attacks on isolated Tutsi communities as practice runs for the final solution. More often than not, it simply involved spreading the word of hatred far and wide.

Before we travel on, it is instructive to consider Rwandan history and the precise definitions – in so much as there can be precision – of the words 'Hutu' and 'Tutsi'. For if I learned anything in Rwanda it is that a 'pure' ethnic divide is a myth. In southern Rwanda in particular there was extensive intermarrying between Tutsis and Hutus, and, as I shall detail later, there is a long history of people exchanging identities. The leader of the Interahamwe militia, Robert Kajuga, was a Tutsi whose father had succeeded in changing the family's identity to Hutu.

The historical records indicate that Rwanda's first inhabitants were hunter–gatherers, more commonly known as Twa, or pygmies. Successive migrations from north and east brought groups of farmers and cattle herders. Eventually one clan of cattle herders, members of what is now called the Tutsi tribe, appear to have succeeded in dominating much of the centre of what is now known as Rwanda. As the centuries advanced this clan consolidated its power, although in custom and tradition it absorbed much of the culture of the Hutu farmers it dominated. Today Tutsi and Hutu share a common language, diet and cultural heritage.

What separated Tutsi and Hutu in the past was primarily a matter of occupation and wealth. Thus the Tutsi clan owned large herds of cattle, while their Hutu subjects farmed the land and the Twa subsisted on what they could gather in field and forest. As time progressed many Hutus bought cattle and were assimilated into the Tutsi aristocracy. Some Tutsis became poor and lost their privileged position. In pre-colonial Rwandan society – as in so many other parts of the world – cattle were identified with wealth. Ownership of large herds of cattle allowed the Tutsi nobility to raise armies and to draw vast numbers of Hutus into the web of clientelism (for example, a Hutu peasant would be given a cow, in return for which he would make himself available for work on the land of his patron). Not every Tutsi landowner exploited his Hutu vassals, but there evolved over time a dangerous sense of second-class citizenship among the Hutus. The Tutsi nobility that dominated the centre of Rwanda stressed the importance of physical stature, that is, they claimed their tallness and aquiline facial features were synonymous with superiority. Those who were short and stocky, who worked the land, and who had neither cattle nor ties to the nobility became a distinct second class in Rwandan society.

Journalists who have interviewed Hutu peasants have frequently been told that Tutsis look down on them as 'subhumans'. Any peasants who opposed the evolving order were treated with unmitigated harshness. Tutsi nobles showed no hesitation in massacring the occupants of rebellious villages and confiscating their property. A peasant farmer would be advised to bide his time, to save what he could in the hope of someday purchasing enough cattle to allow for his assimilation into the ruling class. He did not need to be tall or slim to gain entrance into the higher ranks of society: in that sense pre-colonial Rwandan society was solidly materialistic. But the economic realities tended to keep the majority of Hutus in a subject position, whatever their aspirations.

It suited the early colonists to believe in and foster the myth of the Tutsis as black Aryans, men not too dissimilar to Europeans, more noble than savage, who could be trusted to carry out the orders of the white men. Thus grew up the notion of Tutsis (described as Hamites by the colonists) as proto-Europeans, pastoralists who had come down from the north, possibly Ethiopia, into the dark and savage lands in the heart of Africa to impose their superior civilization. The truth is that nobody really knows where the Tutsi clans came from, but it probably wasn't Ethiopia and certainly nowhere remotely close to Europe. The obsession with physical appearance, aided and abetted by the Tutsi ruling class, led the Europeans to all manner of humiliating folly: measuring of skulls and noses and all the discredited junk of the race theorists who thrived in the heyday of African colonialism. One Belgian doctor wrote:

The Hamites ... have a distant, reserved, courteous and elegant manner ... The rest of the population is Bantu, the Bahutu. They are negroes with all the negroid characteristics ... they are childish in nature, both timid and lazy, and as often as not, extremely dirty.

The respected American writer John Gunther, whose book *Inside Africa* contains a wealth of information on pre-independence Africa, visited Rwanda in 1954. His description of the Tutsi ruling class in Rwanda, while repeating the Ethiopian myth, gives an interesting flavour of the atmosphere of the time.

They are not negroes though they may be jet black. A Hamitic or Nilotic people, they were pastoral nomads and cattlemen who came down from the north, and they startlingly resemble Ethiopians – except that I have never seen an Ethiopian seven feet tall ... they are proud, sophisticated and not particularly energetic. Several times we saw Watutsi lords sitting on bicycles and being pushed by their vassals ... no anthropologist has ever explained why the Watutsi are so tall. Possibly diet has something to do with it. In any case tallness is the symbol of racial exclusiveness and pure blood.

The 'Ethiopian factor' was to be a recurring theme in much of the journalistic and academic analysis of the Tutsi/ Hutu divide. In more recent times the Africa correspondent of the *Los Angeles Times*, David Lamb, gave this description of the population of Rwanda's neighbour Burundi (the ethnic mix is roughly the same as in Rwanda, 80 per cent Hutu, 15 per cent Tutsi and 5 per cent Twa):

The short stocky Hutus ... are mostly farmers of Bantu stock, with dark, Negroid features. The Watutsi, who migrated to Burundi in the sixteenth and seventeenth centuries from the north, probably Ethiopia, are cattle people; they are tall, sometimes well over six feet, with long, narrow facial features and their skin is slightly lighter than that of most Africans.

The references to Ethiopia, the inference that the Tutsi were immigrants, were to recur frequently in the period leading up to the genocide and during the killings. Senior Hutu extremists would exhort their followers to send the Tutsis 'back to the Ethiopia' via the nearest river. This was one reason why rivers became such passageways of death during the massacres. The Hutus were, as can be seen from the Gunther extract, cast in the role of dumb serfs. I never saw any evidence in Rwanda or Burundi to support the proposition that Tutsis were lighter skinned than Hutus. Like much else that has been written about the two groups, it appears to be fanciful nonsense, a carry-over from the colonial era. The downgrading of the Hutu peasantry into a subclass was reinforced by the colonial education system and a political structure which placed the king, or Mwaami (a Tutsi of course), at the top and layers of Tutsi notables below him.

An early Belgian colonial film – paid for by the government in Brussels – described the Hutu as creatures with 'souls sad and passive, ignoring all thought for the morrow'. These were people who regarded 'their Tutsi overlords as demi-gods'. The implication of Belgian policy and public utterance was clear enough: the Hutus were a peasant majority and in no way suitable partners in the exploitation of Rwanda. By contrast the Tutsis, with their elitist background, were a minority who had every interest in keeping the country in its existing state. For the colonists it was a perfect partnership.

What had existed prior to the colonists' arrival was a society in which the rich – most of them drawn from the Tutsi nobility, though not exclusively – ruled and the peasants toiled. It suited the interests of the colonists to rule through the existing Tutsi elite, who showed themselves to be willing and compliant, more interested in the preservation of privilege and material wealth than in any question of national identity. In return for their co-operation in imposing the writ of the Germans and later the Belgians, the Tutsi overlords were given extended powers over the lives of the Hutus. In practice this allowed many minor Tutsi chiefs to exploit their Hutu 'subjects' and demand higher contributions of their crops and longer working hours.

The introduction in 1933 of a mandatory identity card system deepened social divisions. Every Rwandan citizen was obliged to carry the card, which stated his name and ethnic identity, i.e. Tutsi, Hutu or Twa. It was similar to the passbook system of South African apartheid except that it predated it by more than a decade. Once labelled, a citizen could not change his or her identity, except with the connivance of a sympathetic or corrupt official. The possibility of elevating oneself from the peasant classes to the aristocracy through the purchase of cattle was removed. Prior to this even the Belgians went along with the notion of allocating ethnic identity on the basis of cattle ownership. One census was conducted by counting the number of cows owned by each family. Hutus with a respectable number of cows were designated Tutsis. But after the introduction of the ID card system a Hutu was a Hutu for life. Hutus were in effect told that their mission in life was to toil (forced labour on the lands of Tutsi nobles was commonplace) and serve in perpetuity. When the northern Hutu – who had largely escaped the writ of Tutsi overlordship before the arrival of the colonists – revolted in the early part of the century they were subdued mercilessly by the Germans and their Tutsi allies. The suppression of that revolt, and the bitter memories which lingered down the years, helped to make northern Rwanda a hotbed of Hutu nationalism. It is no surprise that many of those who came to dominate Rwandan politics after the first stage of independence, including President Habyarimana and his in-laws, came from the north.

But the equations of power and patronage began to change dramatically in the years leading up to independence.

The moves towards self-determination were under way across the continent of Africa, and the Belgians began to look warily at their current partners in the ruling and exploitation of Rwanda. The Tutsis who had served their purpose well in the heyday of colonial power began to look very unpromising as potential rulers of a future independent Rwanda. Anything like a free vote would mean the end of Tutsi rule and the influence of the Belgians. To add to their fears the Belgians found themselves facing an increasingly confrontational attitude from the Tutsi-dominated National Rwandese Union (Union Nationale Ruandaise, or UNAR). This party was also positioning itself for the post-independence battle for power and was keen to create a distance between itself and the former colonial masters. The Belgians came to recognize the inevitability of Hutu rule, promptly switched sides and began to support the PARMEHUTU (The Party for the Emancipation of the Hutus). Thus when the Tutsi monarch Mwaami Rudahigwa died in 1959 and Hutus rose in rebellion the Belgians did little or nothing to save the lives of the besieged Tutsis. Estimates of the number of Tutsis killed vary between ten and one hundred thousand. Whatever the true figure, the rivers filled with bodies and tens of thousands of refugees fled the country. The style of killing – stabbing, clubbing, the burning of huts – was almost exactly the same as that used over three decades later. Bertrand Russell described the slaughter as the 'most horrible and systematic human massacre we have had occasion to witness since the extermination of the Jews by the Nazis'.

In neighbouring Burundi the Tutsi minority succeeded in holding power after independence. The population balance might have been more or less the same, but the Tutsis of Burundi dominated the military and used their power to crush Hutu political aspirations. The Burundian army murdered nearly a quarter of a million Hutus (virtually the entire educated class) in 1972. There have been regular crackdowns through the years. In 1992 the Burundian army rampaged through Hutu areas on a murder campaign following a series of attacks by Hutu militiamen. The brutal campaign drove thousands of Hutu refugees into Rwanda. Many of these refugees were later to play a major role in the genocide. They were among the most feared killers and Tutsi survivors spoke of the Burundian refugees' need to humiliate their victims before murdering them. But inside Burundi, in spite of moves towards democratization, the Tutsi-dominated army remains the final arbiter of power. Fearful of suffering the same fate as Rwanda's Tutsis, the Burundian army has used tactics of terror similar to Rwanda's presidential guard.

Many of the Rwandan Tutsis who became refugees in 1959 and 1962 fled to Uganda, settling in the south and centre of the country. There as many as 200,000 people attempted to create new lives in a country that itself was experiencing a traumatic evolution into nationhood. They left with bitter memories and a burning desire to one day come back. Their country of exile was to suffer the terror of rule by Milton Obote (twice) and Idi Amin. A substantial proportion of the Tutsi refugees settled in the Luwero triangle, an area singled out for particularly cruel treatment by both Amin's and Obote's forces. The experience of terror at the hands of the Ugandan army convinced the refugees that their only future lay within Rwanda. Many of their children joined the National Resistance Army of Yoweri Museveni, which eventually overthrew the government of Obote in 1986. Museveni's army had a reputation for discipline and military professionalism, and many of the senior commanders were Rwandan Tutsis. These 'children of '59' regrouped after the end of the Ugandan war and formed into the RPF, determined to return to the country of their forefathers.

In their absence Rwanda followed the well-trodden, post-independence path to a corrupt one-party state. The average citizen had a subsistence existence. The PARME-HUTU elite siphoned off vast sums in public funds and turned the civil service into a party jobs machine. Clientelism thrived, and discrimination against Tutsis was widespread and systematic. There were occasional violent pogroms throughout the sixties, which was a period of fear and uncertainty in Rwanda. Attacks by bands of Tutsi guerrillas (nicknamed *inyenzi*, or 'cockroaches', by the government) led to vicious reprisals. In one such pogrom in 1963 Hutu militias murdered an estimated 10,000 Tutsis.

There was a further outbreak in 1967 – again the Tutsis were butchered and dumped in the rivers – and then a large-scale purge of Tutsis from the universities in 1973. This expanded into a wider pogrom designed to drive the minority from all of the country's educational institutions. As violence spread throughout the country the army's chief of staff, Juvénal Habyarimana, stepped in and staged a *coup d'état* under the pretext of restoring order. Instigating violence and then staging a *coup* in order to quell the same violence is a favoured tactic among potential dictators. It is widely suspected that Habyarimana was behind the 1973 disturbances. Whatever his motives, Habyarimana's rule did not, as many Tutsis had feared, precipitate a total onslaught against the minority. On the contrary, Habyarimana appeared to go out of his way to stress national unity and appealed for an end to ethnic bloodletting. But behind the scenes Habyarimana simply swopped the old southern and central power elite of the PARMEHUTU for his own northern cronies. The northern Hutus, as mentioned earlier, were the most fierce ethnic chauvinists in Rwanda. This had much to do with their experience at the hands of the Germans and their Tutsi allies, who subdued the north in the early part of the century. In power Habyarimana may not have murdered the Tutsis with the same fervour as his predecessors but he was relentless in the task of discrimination and scapegoating. While he and his family and friends filled foreign bank accounts with the country's wealth, the position of the

Rwandan peasantry went from bad to worse. Vast sums of aid sent by foreign governments and agencies went either directly or indirectly into the pockets of senior government ministers and officials. Habyarimana's party, the National Revolutionary Movement for Development (Mouvement Révolutionnaire National pour le Développement, or MRND), dedicated itself to the enrichment of the northern Hutu elite while the peasants were encouraged to blame the Tutsis for their problems. Again there are echoes of the Nazis' scapegoating of the Jews in the thirties. While the president and his cronies grew fat the economic situation steadily worsened. Rwanda is one of the smallest countries in the world, with a land area of just over 26,000 kilometres. The population density is the highest in Africa. As many as 400 people are in theory dependent on each square kilometre of land. But this has not prevented Rwandans from being able to feed themselves throughout most of the country's years of independence. A heavy population density does not necessarily translate into the kind of famine witnessed in countries like Sudan and Ethiopia. Rwanda has rich soil and a plentiful supply of rainfall. When famine or severe hunger has taken place it has been largely due to factors such as war or external economic pressures. For example the coffee price (coffee accounted for 75 per cent of Rwanda's export earnings) collapsed in 1989 and led to severe hardship for hundreds of thousands of farmers. The ongoing war with the RPF since 1990 caused huge population movements, disturbing the fragile economic balance in the areas that had experienced the influx of refugees. The upheavals increased the competition for scarce resources and made the mass of Hutu peasants fearful for the security of their land. The extremists told them repeatedly that the Tutsis were coming to seize their land. In reality the thieving of resources was being done by Habyarimana and his cronies. But western donors increased pressure for some kind of economic and political account-ability. Slowly but surely the wealth tap was shut off; the money and jobs that had been used to buy the loyalty of the military and the civil service were in danger of disap-pearing. The implications of any democratization of society were horrifying to the elite: without political power the whole system of patronage and clientelism would collapse.

When guerrillas of the Tutsi-dominated RPF staged their offensive in 1990 the Habyarimana regime seized the opportunity for a major and dangerous exercise in scape-goating. Aware of mounting discontent in the countryside, the president and the entire organizational machinery of the MRND and military began to actively foment fear and hatred of the Tutsis. By this stage Tutsis living within Rwanda were already heavily penalized: there were only two Tutsi members of parliament, only one Tutsi town mayor, no Tutsi regional mayors and only one Tutsi ambassador. There were almost no Tutsis in the army and the police. To even vaguely imply that they were still a privileged elite was plainly ludicrous. However, Habyar-imana and his clique (known as the Akazu, or 'little hut') began to build up a civilian militia – the Interahamwe, or 'Those who stand together' – which, with the army and the presidential guard, would be used to protect MRND power and privilege. The theory behind the anti-Tutsi propaganda was simple: rather than lose power to a growing opposition movement led by Hutu moderates and including Tutsis, the MRND would drag the old bogey out of the closet and direct the anger of the poor in the direction of the Tutsis. This would provide the people with a pressure valve and remove, literally, any potent opposition to MRND rule. Privilege would be maintained albeit at the expense of fomenting ethnic hatred. It is not known whether Habyarimana intended the killing to reach the scale that it did after his death. What can be said is that he encouraged the most virulent anti-Tutsi propaganda and that, given Rwanda's history, he must have been aware of the potential consequences. There had also been a growing number of attacks on Tutsis inside Rwanda between 1989 and the actual start of the genocide in April 1994. Habyarimana did nothing to quell the violence that was being instigated by his henchmen in the militia and army. Hutu extremism was essentially a useful tool by which the corrupt elite that ran the country could hold on to power.

Habyarimana might have been able to ride the tiger and survive had the weight of international pressure and the RPF's growing military strength not forced him to compromise. Having treated earlier ceasefire and democracy agreements with contempt, he was finally forced to concede the principle of multi-party politics in 1991. A number of political parties were formed, including the Democratic Republican Movement (Mouvement Démocratique Républicain, or MDR), whose members were singled out for particularly vicious treatment later on. The MDR represented a credible, Hutu-dominated opposition to Habyarimana. He responded by accusing opposition political groups of acting as the lackeys of the RPF, and he tacitly encouraged the setting up of the Hutu extremist Coalition for the Defence of the Republic – a breakaway of the ruling party that was in a position to propagate virulent anti-Tutsi policies at a publicly safe distance from Habyarimana. It is vital to remember that while publicly proclaiming himself willing to reform the president was privately financing and helping to organize the Hutu extremist militias. Any true democratization of Rwanda could conceivably have seen Habyarimana and his allies facing trial for their part in earlier purges against the Tutsis and their political opponents. In February 1993 an offensive by the RPF considerably weakened the president's negotiating position. The RPF moved towards Kigali and might have seized the city had French troops not intervened on the side of the government.

The French had long supported Habyarimana and had no wish to see him driven from power by the rebels. The pro-Habyarimana faction in Paris was led by François Mitterrand's son Jean-Christophe, who saw Rwanda as part

of a Francophone Africa under threat from the encroach-
ments of the English-speaking nations to the north and
east, i.e. Uganda and Tanzania. Among Jean-Christophe's
gifts to the Rwandan president was the personal jet that
was shot out of the sky on 6 April. The implication of
this friendship was clear: if the price for maintaining some
degree of French influence was the preservation of despots
and kleptocrats, then Paris was always more than willing
to pay. In contrast to Habyarimana the leaders of the RPF
were largely English-speaking. The long years of exile in
Uganda had forced the Tutsi refugees to abandon the
French language. For their part the French maintained a
military mission and a sizeable detachment of intelligence
officers in Rwanda. With their contacts inside the army
and at every level of government and the state media, Paris
could not have been ignorant of the genocidal intentions of
many of the senior officers and officials. For the French to
suggest otherwise would be a lamentable comment on the
abilities of their own intelligence services and diplomats.

However, French assistance was not enough to save Habyarimana's regime from the combined effects of RPF military
pressure and international agitation for democratization.
By having seized the military initiative the RPF was
ultimately able to force Habyarimana into negotiations
that culminated in the Arusha Peace Accords of August
1993. The ten-day talks at Arusha in Tanzania produced a
series of protocols, the most significant of which were

those on power-sharing, a dramatic reduction in the powers of the presidency and, crucially, the integration of the RPF into the armed forces. The rebels were to provide 40 per cent of the troops for the army lower ranks and 50 per cent of the officer corps. Under huge international pressure Habyarimana put his signature to the accords. Although he still did everything in his power to split the opposition and maintain absolute power, the domestic and international pressure was too much. Almost every international representative who met him in the weeks leading up to his assassination sensed that Habyarimana was coming to terms – albeit unwillingly – with reality: either share power or face war with the RPF and international isolation.

The Arusha Peace Accords were to be his death warrant. The extremists he had cultivated and the men who had grown rich during the days of the one-party state were not about to see their privilege disappear with the stroke of a pen. Now, instead of holding fast, Habyarimana was weakening, threatening to pull the house down around them. It was time to install a more reliable man. On the evening of 6 April, as Habyarimana was returning from a session of negotiations at Arusha, two missiles were fired at his jet as it landed at Kigali International Airport. The most likely explanation – one disputed by Hutu extremists and their French supporters – is that soldiers of the presidential guard based next to the airport fired the missiles. There is another theory that members of the French military or security services, or mercenaries in the pay of France, shot down the aircraft. Although no firm proof has been produced, there are senior figures in the Belgian security services who think the French may have wanted rid of Habyarimana, believing he was about to hand the country over to the RPF. The jet crashed into the grounds of the presidential palace, which is close to the airport. Habyarimana was killed, along with the president of Burundi, Cyprien Ntaryamira and the chief of staff of Rwanda's army, Deogratias Nsabimana. The MRND government immediately blamed the RPF – and, by extension, all Tutsis – for the killing, suggesting that somehow RPF soldiers had managed to locate themselves next to the biggest army base in the country and murder the president. It was possible, of course, but highly improbable. The RPF had Habyarimana where it wanted him: weak and increasingly susceptible to pressure. On the other hand the army and the extremists had every reason to be rid of him: his death would create a political vacuum that would be filled by an interim government made up of Hutu extremists. Such a government would be in a position to disavow all agreements reached by its predecessor. The days of privilege would return. More importantly, the murder of the president would provide the perfect pretext for implementing the final solution of the Tutsi problem, as well as for the destruction of moderate Hutu opposition politicians. The army and the militias were ready with lists of their enemies; the extremist radio stations and newspapers had already created an atmosphere of anti-Tutsi hysteria. All that remained was for the signal to be given. No sooner had Habyarimana's jet been shot down than the killings began in earnest. The one hundred days of genocide had been launched.

In my journey through Rwanda I encountered many of the killers: the genocide was a crime of mass complicity, one could hardly avoid meeting people who had been involved. They stood at every roadblock, at every army encampment; they loitered around every municipal building. A few gave the appearance of being truly psychopathic individuals. The mass of others were ragged and illiterate peasants easily roused to hatred of the Tutsis. Perhaps the most sinister people I met were the educated political elite, men and women of charm and sophistication who spoke flawless French and who could engage in long philosophical debates about the nature of war and democracy. But they shared one thing in common with the soldiers and the peasants: they were drowning in the blood of their fellow countrymen. Before you read this book and while you read it, remember the figures, never ever forget them: *in one hundred days up to one million people were hacked, shot, strangled, clubbed and burned to death. Remember, carve this into your consciousness: one million.* This is not to ignore the vast numbers who were wounded, raped and terrorized, or the thousands of orphans whom I found clustered around derelict buildings across the country. In our world of instant televised horror it can become easy to see a black body in almost abstract terms, as part of the huge smudge of eternally miserable blackness that has loomed in and out of the public mind through the decades: Biafra in the sixties; Uganda in the seventies; Ethiopia in the eighties; and now Rwanda in the nineties. We are fed a diet of starving children, of stacked corpses and battalions of refugees, and in the end we find ourselves despising the continent of Africa because it haunts and shames us. A year before the Rwanda genocide occurred I was sitting in the BBC radio studio in Johannesburg taking part in the annual correspondents' review of the year. The subject of Central Africa came up and I spoke about the increasing danger of a catastrophe somewhere in the region – I wrongly imagined that the source of disaster would be Zaire, where President Mobutu's grip on power seemed to be faltering. A London-based correspondent wondered aloud why we should care about disputes in obscure countries. I was taken aback by the question, believing that it reflected a narrow view of the world and the issues and emotions that shape our collective history. I answered by saying – and I hold passionately to this view today – that we should care because we belong to the same brotherhood of man as the citizens of seemingly remote African countries. It is not a political reason and some may call it naïve. That is their prerogative. For me, however, the conclusion is unavoidable: genocidal killing in Africa diminishes all of us.

CHAPTER ONE

Travellers

The road south is narrow and endless. We have been driving since early morning, and the green hill country has begun to lose focus. It is a blur on to which have been painted occasional villages in shades of muddy brown and the burned yellow of banana thatch. At each Ugandan village small boys run to the edge of the road, offering cokes and bananas for sale. Some of them thrust skewers of burned meat, rancid and charcoal black, through the window. At first we found them entertaining, almost dancing in front of us, cheering excitedly as we approached. Now, seven hours later, they are tiresome, another hazard of the road along with the cattle and goats. Any journey, even towards war, becomes a matter of routine if it goes on long enough. In the distance I see mountains slowly revealing themselves as the rain clouds retreat into the east. Appearing out of the countless smaller hills, these mountains appear fantastically large. 'Those mountains are Rwanda,' says Moses, his head hunched over the steering wheel. Moses Baale is one of our two drivers. He is forty-five years old and once served as a soldier in the army of Idi

Amin. 'I was made to go into the army,' he told me apologetic-
ally. When the Tanzanians invaded Uganda and overthrew
Amin, Moses deserted, hiding his uniform in the bush and
running as fast as he could back to his family. From the outset
Moses has made it clear that he does not want to go to Rwanda.
But his job is to drive people wherever they want to go, and he
has accepted this mission because it is his job. 'Me, I have the
wife and two children back in Kampala. The kids are going to
school,' he says, 'and I need to get money. I am not here
otherwise, believe me.'

Having survived the madness of the Amin years, Moses feels
that he deserves better than dying in Rwanda. We have spent
much of the morning reassuring him, but I sense he does not
believe us. His partner Edward is driving the second Land
Rover. Edward is younger, around twenty-five or twenty-six,
and much less worried about the danger. He constantly asks
about money. How much did the cameras cost? How much do we
get paid? He likes to wear a bowler hat and walks with the half
slouch, half prowl of a city boy. Tall and handsome and
impulsive, Edward does not like taking instructions. Already we
have clashed with him over his driving, urging him not to shoot
ahead of Moses. He listens to us with an expression that is
balanced somewhere between contempt and a grudging acceptance
of our authority. 'Fine, fine, that's just fine,' he says, and
proceeds to drive even faster. But Edward has an advantage over
the rest of us. He has been into Rwanda twice. Just the previous
week he drove down as far as Kigali, through the ruined towns
and the empty villages. Edward saw bodies in the river on the

way to Kigali. 'There is lots of them,' he says. When children try to sell us fish, Edward says not to eat them. They come from Lake Victoria and the fish are said to be feeding on corpses. 'Not nice to eat, bad luck to eat,' he says, smiling.

We had set ourselves the target of getting to Kabale, the Ugandan town nearest the Rwandan border, by nightfall. The plan was to rest overnight and then cross into RPF-controlled territory just after dawn. David was sitting in front of me peering at a road map of Rwanda, drawing his long, spidery finger down through the centre of the country. As the Land Rover bumped and jolted over the rough roads, his body bounced back and forth, but his finger maintained its steady progress down the highway towards Kigali. David was our team leader. At sixty years of age he had lived through the Second World War, been an army officer at Suez and travelled more miles of Africa than any other BBC journalist. Tall and silver-haired, with a narrow, craggy face, David was hard-working and modest, a man who would always see to it that the drivers had eaten before touching food himself, who woke before any of us and worked longer hours than anybody I had ever known. Thus, when he used to shake me awake before dawn with a cheery 'good morning, old chap' and a cup of tea, I could only smile and thank him for rousing me from a deep and comfortable sleep. David rarely allowed his personal feelings to show. I think it was a combination of ingrained reserve and a determination that nothing should deflect him from the job at hand. He also, I suspect, was careful about not communicating any sense of fear to the others in the group. Yet, as we travelled south towards the border, he seemed unusually quiet. The chat and excited conversation of the early part of the journey had evaporated into a prolonged, melancholy silence. Suddenly he turned around and began talking about his two young daughters. They were aged six and eight and the lights of his life. 'Whenever I go somewhere I send them a story about this giant called Walter. They have had the adventures of Walter in South Africa, in China ... Walter has been everywhere. I wonder what adventures he'll have in Rwanda.' 'Here, I have something for you,' I said. I had been reading Yeats during the journey, coming back again and again to the poem 'The Second Coming' with its 'blood-dimmed tide' and 'The ceremony of innocence is drowned'. But for David there was something far more appropriate to the moment. I thumbed the pages until I found 'A Prayer for my Daughter'. David took the book and read:

> Once more the storm is howling, and half hid
> Under this cradle-hood and coverlid
> My child sleeps on. There is no obstacle
> But Gregory's wood and one bare hill
> Whereby the haystack- and roof-levelling wind,
> Bred on the Atlantic, can be stayed;
> And for an hour I have walked and prayed
> Because of the great gloom that is in my mind.

34

I have walked and prayed for this young child an hour
And heard the sea-wind scream upon the tower,
And under the arches of the bridge, and scream
In the elms above the flooded stream;
Imagining in excited reverie
That the future years had come,
Dancing to a frenzied drum,
Out of the murderous innocence of the sea.

He finished and put the book on his lap, and then took off his glasses. Although I could not see his face I thought he was wiping away a tear. Moses noticed this too and a powerful feeling of loneliness seemed to envelop the three of us. Something about seeing David in the thrall of this fatherly emotion made me feel terribly the absence of those I loved. Rwanda was an unknown for us all. We had watched the television pictures and listened to the radio, but there was a huge distance between being a screen spectator and actually going there. The nearer we came to Rwanda, the more pressing the need to remember points of normality: home, garden, pets, books, loved ones. I wondered where my wife was at that moment. Probably visiting a friend in Johannesburg, or walking through a shopping mall, or maybe watching television, waiting for the news reports from Rwanda with a mixture of fascination and dread. She did not want me to go to Rwanda. The night before we left she helped me to pack and in a calm voice told me I was never to go anywhere dangerous again. I made the promise and told her everything would be all right. We would not be going near any dangerous areas. She smiled and pretended to accept this because believing it helped us to prepare for the moment of leave-taking. That night we both lay awake for hours, shifting and turning, unable to anchor down in the restlessness that stretchedandstretchedtowardsdawn.Inthemorning,byagreement, she left the house before me and smiled goodbye, as if we would see each other again that evening. Emotional survival is sometimes based on such necessary fictions.

As we neared Kabale, a couple of white United Nations trucks rumbled past us on their way north to resupply in Kampala. We were watching out for any Ugandan military vehicles. Kampala was alive with rumours that Yoweri Museveni was sending truckloads of weapons – rockets, artillery, heavy machine-guns – to help the RPF. The sieges of Gitarama and Kigali were under way, and the rebels needed more ammunition. The UN was monitoring the border but nobody paid them any serious attention. A handful of unarmed soldiers sitting in the bush with walkie-talkies and binoculars: all they could do was watch and report. Most of the weaponry was going in on forest and mountain tracks that the UN would never get near. Although it was never proved, Museveni had several reasons for supplying the RPF with arms and ammunition. There was the question of a debt of honour: many of the RPF troops had fought on Museveni's side during the Ugandan civil war. Equally important,

Museveni did not want a defeated RPF army returning to Uganda and causing destabilization in the south. A clear victory for the rebels was very much in his interest. Nobody could prove that he was arming the RPF, but everybody believed it.

Periodically the pressure of having to travel slowly and follow behind our vehicle got too much for Edward and he zipped ahead, racing into the dusk, while Glenn and Tony looked out the rear window, all shaking heads and hands raised to heaven.

'What can we do?' mouthed Tony.

'Oh, that fellow. I will speak to him later. I will certainly speak to him,' muttered Moses, who steadfastly refused to increase his speed. Glenn and Tony were white South Africans who had just seen their country march from apartheid to democracy. Both voted for the first time in the April elections and were feeling good about South Africa, no longer ashamed to say where they came from when people asked, as they always did in Africa. At Kampala they were welcomed warmly by the immigration officials. Everybody asked them about Mandela. When they heard that Glenn and Tony had actually filmed the old man, there were compliments and much backslapping.

'Jeeze, man, now I understand what they mean when they talk about coming back to Africa,' grinned Tony, who had spent a good deal of his adult life in self-imposed exile, sick to his teeth of the politics of race. Although they

37

were both white, English-speaking South Africans, Glenn and Tony were remarkably different. Tony was a short-story writer and novelist. He took notes endlessly and was a constant source of pulsing energy. Growing up in the wealthy northern suburbs of Johannesburg, he went to one of South Africa's top public schools, graduated with a degree in English from the University of Cape Town, and then left for the United States when the South African military authorities threatened to draft him for their war in Angola. He met a Japanese woman and went to Tokyo with her, teaching English at an international school until the call of his homeland became too powerful and he returned, just as the ANC was unbanned and Mandela was preparing to lead his people to freedom. Tony was of German descent, with fair hair and sharp blue eyes that were constantly flickering about, taking in everything as if they were enjoying their last few seconds of sight. In height he was the smallest of the group, but with the broad, powerful shoulders he had built up as a college rowing champion, Tony had an imposing physical presence.

Glenn Middleton was born in what was then Rhodesia in the early sixties. His family came to South Africa after his parents split up. To describe his childhood as difficult would be something of an understatement. Among other things he spent time in Boys Town, the correctional facility where the youngsters effectively make and enforce their own law, with the guidance of adults. Glenn went out of choice. His older brother had been sent to Boys Town by the courts, and Glenn could not bear to be separated from him. Later he would say that Boys Town saved him from a life of crime. He grew up there, learned to respect other people and most of all to believe in himself. Later he went to a state school, but he disliked the institution and the enforced tedium of classroom days. At the age of eighteen Glenn was drafted into the army, like most young whites of his age. The military life suited him. He loved the bush and had been around guns since he was a child, hunting for guinea fowl in the cold highveld winters until he became a star marksman. In the army his shooting abilities would normally have ensured his dispatch to the Angolan front line. But the war in Angola was going through one of its quieter phases and Glenn escaped the horrors of the battle-field. Instead the army put him to work as a photographer, a move that was to see him eventually work his way up to being one of the best news cameramen in the country. By the time he joined the BBC he had an impressive reputation for physical courage and having the all important 'eye' – the instinct of vision, the sense of a picture that distinguishes the really good from the average. He was not given to intellectualizing; to those who did not know him he came across in many ways as a prototypical Southern African man, rugby-loving, barbecue-cooking, a son of the outdoors. His greatest interest in life was fishing and he would head for the Indian Ocean coast whenever the South African story quietened down for a few days. Like

Tony he was blond and blue-eyed but his round, open face was quicker to betray emotion. The tough man of the bushveld persona was only one part of Glenn Middleton. There was another much quieter and gentler person at work beneath the surface, a man whose loyalty and kindness I had experienced working in the South African townships. Glenn was the most sensitive cameraman I had ever worked with and when he gazed through the viewfinder he was an artist, quiet in the mastery of his craft. The journey into Rwanda was taking place only two months after the car crash that had claimed the life of our colleague John Harrison. Glenn was driving the car but survived the accident. He was never one for talking aloud about his troubles, but I knew he was suffering intense emotional pain as we set out on our journey.

It was well after nightfall by the time we reached Kabale and found rooms in a small, shambling hotel on the main street. The World Traveller Motel also served as the town's main bar. Unusually for an African drinking establishment it was filled with quiet, sombre-looking men sipping beers who watched us unload our equipment with only passing interest. There was no music and no prostitutes, two of the quintessential elements of Africa's great roads of commerce. It was as if the gloom had seeped over the border from Rwanda like a bad memory: the people of Kabale had known the terror of Obote and Amin. Mass murder was written into their memory. Although they were making money selling petrol, food and beer to the UN, they appeared unsettled by the close presence of death. Most of the customers were lorry drivers taking relief supplies into Rwanda as well as whatever else moved on the dark roads south.

The town's other hotel, the White Horse Inn, was the base for the UN monitors. We found them in the hotel garden, sitting around a barbecue. The meat sizzled and ice clinked in long glasses of beer and wine. The food was being served by a sad-eyed Ugandan. His white chef's uniform was spattered with grease and flecks of animal blood, and he never once looked up as he loaded the food on to our plates. The monitors were a mixed group of Latin Americans and seemed to have little knowledge of what was happening in Rwanda. With their bright t-shirts and baseball caps they might have been attending a party in a fashionable suburb of Rio. They were friendly but could not understand why we were going to Rwanda. The border at Kabale was far enough for them. One African UN soldier, I think he came from Ghana, had been into Rwanda and warned us to be careful. 'The rebels are OK, but they will insist you go with them and that's just as well.' He paused and then spoke again. 'They will tell you that the countryside as far as Kigali is secure but once you get to know them they admit it's not really true. There are lots of militia still hiding out in the swamps and the forest. You wanna be very careful in there.' We had heard these stories about phantom bands of Interahamwe already. In

Nairobi on our way through there were endless warnings from our colleagues about the militia.

That night we crammed into two small rooms, hauling our cameras and innumerable pieces of equipment up the narrow, shaky stairs of the hotel. The beds were clean. No bugs or lice that could be seen. Glenn produced a South African spray that he swore would keep us safe from mosquitoes throughout the night. He sprayed a thick cloud of the chemical in both rooms, and I drifted to sleep with a sharp stinging in my nose and eyes. But in the clammy dark they whined and dived above our heads. I was too tired to fight back and they feasted in the darkness. At around four in the morning I was awoken briefly by the heavy, growling sound of a convoy of lorries driving through. From the direction of the sound it appeared as if they were driving south towards Rwanda. Perhaps they were part of Museveni's alleged resupply effort. Who else would be driving into that country so late at night?

At six David's radio alarm exploded into life and the reassuring strains of 'Lillibullero', the BBC World Service signature tune, flooded the room. The news out of Rwanda was bleak. As the rebels advanced, they were discovering more bodies, thousands of bodies in churches and community halls. The siege of Kigali had intensified and there was frequent mortar and shell fire. At the end of the news David switched off the radio, looked across in my direction and said with classical understatement, 'It should be an interesting few weeks, old boy.' I turned towards the wall for a last few moments' sleep but instead found myself thinking back to something that was said to me by a friend in Nairobi. He had just come out of Rwanda and was sitting at the terrace bar of the Norfolk Hotel, drunk and tired and lapsing from one long silence into another. Around us were groups of tourists either going to, or returning from, safaris in Kenya's national parks. They were happy and excited, exchanging tips on insect repellent, sun burn, the best times of day to see different animals. I wondered if they had heard anything about the genocide taking place a couple of hours' flight away in Rwanda. Occasionally my friend would pipe up and begin to say something about Rwanda but he had passed the stage of drunken fluency. There were now only bursts of words, scrambled and squelched out in an agonizing rant. He knew he was too drunk to make much sense and got up, weaving through the tables towards the hotel lobby. I followed him, guiding him towards the elevator, where he turned to say goodnight. As the lift doors opened, he put his hand on my shoulder and blurted his goodbye message: 'It's in the fucking soul, man . . . spiritual damage is what it is.' When I met him at breakfast the following day, he was sunny and cheerful and made no mention of the previous evening. He was planning to go to Burundi to see if the madness was spreading out of Rwanda across the border. I did not know if he remembered last night's words, and I thought better of asking him to explain them.

But in the small Ugandan hotel, in the quiet before we

rose to begin our journey, his words were playing over and over again in my head. Strange talk even in drink. *The soul. Spiritual damage.* As a group foreign correspondents are not given to discussions of a metaphysical or existential nature. We are trained in the school of the present, taught to analyse the tangible. There are men and women with spiritual beliefs, but these are rarely if ever discussed with colleagues. I could only conclude that something had changed inside my friend. Something that he had seen or experienced, perhaps the collected images of weeks, had prompted this hard-headed reporter to contemplate the soul of man.

I was roused from my thoughts by a young girl who had come to the door with a bucket of hot water. One by one we shaved and washed and packed our bags. The hotel's other guests were wandering about in a narrow courtyard, sharing a large pail of hot water. There were three, all of them lorry drivers, big men stripped to the waist in the morning chill. I passed the door of one of the men I had seen drinking the night before. He was sitting on the bed, a woman buttoning his shirt with one hand, stroking his head with the other. On the floor beside them was nearly a bottle of beer. Another woman, wrapped in a grey blanket, stood apart from them, fiddling with a transistor radio. She looked up and caught my eye. I smiled but she ignored the gesture and went on playing with the radio. It refused to be coaxed into life. Then the man turned his head and, spotting me, gave a wide grin,

44

nodding from woman to woman as he did so. I said good morning and continued on towards the courtyard, where David had begun his ritual of making morning tea. We drank and ate our dried biscuits in silence. Afterwards we trooped out and saw that a thick mist had come down overnight and spread itself like a curtain across the road south to Rwanda.

CHAPTER TWO

Rebels

So beautiful to watch and listen. We have stopped yards from the border and in the earliness and quiet the sun is slowly burning the mist off the hillsides, revealing the country that had been hidden from us in the night. At first we can make out only the nearest trees and banana plants, strange shapes like wings sprouting out of the mist. Somewhere among the banana groves there are birds singing, bright and curious. Glenn starts to mimic the call of the birds: long sharp whistles that climb in pitch at the end of each call. The imitation is intensely real and within seconds the birds are answering back. Glenn tells us he learned to do this as a child in the African bush. Looking at him, crouched in the thick grass at the edge of the road, I feel a sense of security. He is a white man like me but he is of Africa. I can sense his ease in the bush. It does not hold the same threat for him as it does for me. The trees and the tall grass and scrub are part of the same short word that begins at the Cape of Good Hope and rambles all the way to the Mediterranean — Africa, Africa, Africa. I have lived on this continent for four years, have been visiting it for more than a decade, but I am a stranger here in a way that Glenn and Tony are not. I know that I will be depending on them in the weeks ahead. It is they who have made all the practical preparations, packing the tents and the food, buying the jerrycans of petrol and dealing with the assorted rogues of Nairobi and Kampala, passing sweets and money to the shadow children who flicker around us in every town and village with their hands outstretched. Christ, I am nervous. If we are turned back now I won't give a toss. Coming down to the border in the mist, my mind has been unable to shake away the words of my drunken friend in Nairobi. What is he talking about . . . spiritual damage? As I think about this the name 'Rwanda' – say it again, RWANDA – has begun to swell in my imagination. Then there is a knock on the window of the jeep. It is David, smiling and holding out my passport. 'Come on, chaps, on with the show.' His voice trails off as he walks back to the second car. Then Moses and Edward start the engines and we are moving forward and I know that I cannot stop now. The barrier lifts and Uganda slips away.

Just inside the border there were some twisted and rusting signs. They reminded us to drive on the right. We had passed from Anglophone to Francophone Africa. The European Union had paid some of the cost of this highway in the days when the late President Habyarimana was still soaking up vast sums in foreign aid. It was a well-made tar road and stretched south to Kigali before breaking off in different directions to Burundi, Tanzania and Zaire. A few months ago this was one of the great arteries of Central Africa. It carried trucks full of goods for the markets of Rwanda, buses crammed with peasants and itinerant traders, Land Rovers of white overland travellers, some of them heading as far south as Johannesburg and Cape Town. It had been the highway of migrant workers and university students heading to Bujumbura, Butare and Kigali. A few months ago the road had literally hummed and vibrated with the traffic of several nations. On the day we arrived it was empty. Nothing moved or breathed anywhere that we could see. The only traffic now was relief trucks and whatever the RPF was rolling down to besieged Kigali. In the previous few weeks the highway had been witness to a vast human exodus. Tens of thousands of Hutus fled south towards Kigali, the rebels in angry pursuit. Now the roadside grasses were sprouting in every direction, leaning out into the highway so that they brushed the windows of our cars. The rains had brought forth a great tangle of vegetation. With nobody to cultivate the fields the weeds and wild grasses were sweeping across the countryside. In less than five minutes we had gone from a country where people were going out into the fields, gathering wood, cooking food, walking and enjoying the new morning, to a place where nothing stirred. Only the breeze rising occasionally to flatten the rampant grasses and the steady growl of our diesel engines interrupted the silence. It was as if a giant Hoover had been directed down from the heavens and sucked away everything that moved.

Apart from that immense silence I can recall two things very vividly about those first moments inside Rwanda: there were thousands of yellow and white flowers, peeking out from the grassy wilderness, and hovering above them wave after wave of white butterflies, dancing in the indescribable quiet of a country where nobody was home.

The contrast with Uganda left Moses feeling fidgety. He shared his family home in a crowded suburb of Kampala with an assortment of relatives and in-laws. This kind of emptiness was something he had not been prepared for. He began to tap his fingers on the steering wheel, a gesture of nervousness with which we would become familiar in the weeks ahead. I did not know, could hardly imagine, the things Moses must have seen during his days fighting for Idi Amin. He was such a gentle and softspoken man that it was hard to see him in a soldier's uniform, a man serving one of the most ruthless dictators in African history. Once on the journey down I had asked him if he knew anything about Makindye, the notorious torture house where Amin's Bureau of State Research (the secret police) had butchered his political and tribal opponents, clubbing them over the head to save money on ammunition. Moses said he knew the place but had never worked there. He would take me to visit there some day if I wanted. I was inclined to believe that he had not worked as a political executioner. Probably like so many other soldiers I had met in the service of dictators the length and breadth of Africa, Moses had simply needed the job. Being of the same tribe as

Amin was a passport into the military where food, clothing and accommodation were guaranteed, whatever about regular pay. All Moses would say about Amin was that he was 'mad . . . real, real mad'.

Then, without warning, Moses slammed on the brakes. He had seen them first. A group of around twenty in full camouflage uniforms, automatic rifles at the ready. 'RPF, RPF,' he whispered, slowly bringing the car back into first gear and driving in the direction of the group of soldiers. They were lanky, thin and most looked like teenagers. But as we got closer I noticed that their uniforms were neat, and that the troops themselves were not slouching, but instead seemed to be standing to attention. An older soldier detached himself from the group and waved us down, pointing towards a low customs building that lay immediately around the bend from where the troops were positioned. The grass had recently been cleared back from the roadside near here, and there was no sign of the usual detritus of beer bottles and discarded clothing that follows so many African guerrilla armies. As we slowed to a halt, David began to rummage in his bag. 'Nothing to be concerned about, chaps, they know we're coming. I went to see them in Brussels and the chap there said he'd send a fax,' he said. 'They said they'd send a fax?' I asked disbelievingly, 'a fax to some camp in the middle of Africa?' I groaned as David fished out a sheaf of documents from his bag. I knew he was a highly organized man but the idea that our immediate well-being depended on the possibility of a fax being sent from the Belgian capital to a rebel-held border post was difficult to believe. There had been several stories in the past week about journalists turning up unannounced at the rebel headquarters, only to be sent back to Kampala to begin the process of contacting the RPF all over again. Two RPF minders had been detailed to meet us in Kampala but they had never arrived. What chance then that there really existed a piece of paper that would allow us to go on? Having taken the first step across the border into Rwanda, I now had every intention of travelling on.

We all climbed out of the vehicles and walked towards the customs post. An RPF soldier came forward and introduced himself as a lieutenant. 'So you must be the gentlemen from the BBC . . . We have received your fax and the commissar of information is waiting for you down at Mulindi . . . welcome.' He smiled and extended his hand to each of us in turn. 'See, I told you we'd be fine. Just trust in me, chaps,' said David, as he handed over our passports and business cards. Within a few minutes we had signed our names in the RPF's visitors' book, had our passports returned, and were driving down the road under escort to the army's headquarters in the tea fields of Mulindi.

The young soldier who was our guide said nothing on the way down. He must have been a recent recruit because he spoke no English, unlike the older RPF cadres who had grown up in Uganda. He was wearing the standard combat fatigues – dark sand colour with flecks of jungle green – and a pair of wellington boots. 'The boots, where did you get the boots?' I asked, pointing at his feet. He began to grin and, unable to answer my question, stroked the shiny rubber, nodding his head vigorously. As we passed along the road, I noticed more and more young troops appearing, all of them wearing wellingtons. I heard later that the rebels had overrun a warehouse, where they found thousands of pairs of boots. As they clomped along in the heat the boy soldiers looked curiously innocent in their shiny new boots. In two days they would be at the front line, in Kigali or Gitarama or one of the other places of killing.

Lieutenant Frank Ndore strolled down the rutted track and held out his hand. 'I am your escort . . . I listen to the BBC all the time . . . *Newshour* on World Service . . . dah dah dah.' He began to sing the programme's signature tune. Frank had lively, bright eyes set in a thin face, across which stretched a thick black moustache, giving him the appearance of a Latin American guerrilla fighter who had somehow rambled into an African war. Frank wore his beret at a slightly rakish angle, but his fatigues were immaculate and his leather combat boots were shining. He was thin and wiry, not as tall or tough-looking as the other soldiers who stood near by; but from their deferential attitude I immediately formed the impression that Frank Ndore was a man to be reckoned with. I noticed that he was a missing a thumb on his right hand. Frank spotted my curiosity. 'That happened up in the mountains, back in 1990 when we first came through. I got shot in the hand . . . that was it, lost the thumb. That was nothing. A lot of men and women I knew were killed in the fighting. The thumb really was nothing.' He spoke in such a matter-of-fact, deliberate tone that I could believe the loss of the digit had been easily rationalized as a very minor casualty of war.

It had been nearly midday by the time we reached the RPF headquarters at Mulindi and met up with Frank. The headquarters seemed virtually empty. The military leadership had reportedly moved south towards Kigali in the past few days to be nearer the front. I say 'reportedly' because the RPF never ever revealed the location of its senior military and political commanders. Several senior commanders had been killed in the 1990 offensive, and the organization was consciously keeping them out of the firing line, concerned now that they should have enough senior men and women to form a government in the near future. The Mulindi camp had been a tea estate since colonial days, but nothing had been harvested there for several seasons. Driving in, we had passed through wild thickets of tea that were slowly advancing on to the dirt track. As far as the eye could see great tracts of tea plantation sprouted in the fertility that had come with the rains. Frank told us that the tea estate provided an ideal base camp. It was near the border, easily guarded and there were plenty of administrative offices to house the RPF's

54

leadership. As Frank continued with his briefing the sun rose and rose until it was directly overhead and beating into the centre of my brain. 'Can we move out of the sun, Frank?' I gasped out the words. Frank took a long serious look at me and then burst out laughing. 'Where we are going to be travelling you will want to look up at the sun every hour to remind yourself there is a heaven,' he said. Then he put his hand on my shoulder and guided me into the shade of what had once been the main office building of the plantation. 'Only joking, man ... everything on this trip will be just fine,' he added, injecting as much reassurance as he could into the last two words. Once in the shade David Harrison produced a large map of Rwanda, purchased a week before in some small travel agent's office in Brussels. At that moment, standing in an abandoned tea plantation in Central Africa, it was hard to visualize a city like Brussels, where people in suits were sitting in offices, gazing out at a spring afternoon, and thinking about the day that was passing or the night ahead; thinking about lives in which the woes of their country's former colony would remain unutterably distant.

As David and Frank began a protracted discussion about the various routes we might take, I walked over to where Glenn and Tony were talking to a soldier who cannot have been much older than sixteen, perhaps seventeen at a stretch. 'Meet Valence, the boy soldier,' said Tony. If Frank's uniform was a prime example of military neatness, then Valence's was a straightforward fashion statement.

There were razor-like creases in the combat trousers and jacket, a white t-shirt that dazzled in the noon sun, and the same shining boots as the older soldier. But whereas Frank's face was craggy, wise and a little wary, Valence's seemed more like a Boy Scout's than a guerrilla fighter's. He smiled wide warm smiles. Every now and again I could see him catching his own reflection in the wing mirror of one of our jeeps. He liked the sight of himself in uniform. But how did he end up here holding an automatic rifle that was nearly as tall as himself? This boy should be at school, playing football, going out with girls. What personal history brought him here as assistant and bodyguard to Frank? I made a mental note to ask Frank about this once we began travelling. Conversation with Valence proved virtually impossible. He spoke no English, and Glenn and Tony were communicating largely through hand gestures.

Frank called me back to where he and David were standing studying the map. A small, stocky man in a tracksuit who announced himself as the commissar of information had joined them. He repeated Frank's welcome and came straight to the point: 'go wherever you want to but stay out of trouble. Stay away from the fighting at the front and don't get in the way of military operations. But remember to tell the world what has happened here. Show them what has happened. I am sure I do not even need to tell you this.' With that he thanked us for our co-operation, promised to try and arrange interviews with the leaders of the RPF and disappeared through the door of the brick building directly across from where we stood. Other journalists had warned us that the RPF would show us exactly what they wanted us to see. 'They are straight and disciplined and by and large they will tell the truth, but just make sure you get to the other side,' I had been warned. No army in the world wants to show the media the 'other side' of its operations: the civilian dead, the buildings and infrastructure destroyed by indiscriminate shelling, the execution and torture of prisoners. There are journalists who attach themselves to guerrilla armies and begin to see themselves less as reporters than as unarmed propagandists. Far from base, among the company of men who will fight to save your life, who feed you, laugh and cry with you, it is difficult to remain detached. I had felt this before in the mountains of Eritrea, following the hardiest and most determined guerrillas on the African continent, the Eritrean People's Liberation Front, as they fought the terror of Mengistu's Ethiopian army. The Eritreans could claim to have the support of the majority of the local population. It was different for the RPF, which was viewed by most Hutus as a Tutsi army. I broached this with Frank and he began a passionate explanation of the RPF's political position: 'We are not a Tutsi army. We do not care what a person's ethnic origin is. Look around here at Mulindi and tell me if you are able to point out the ethnic origin of every person who is here. Look, some are tall and some are small. What does that say to you? It says nothing except that all over Africa, all over the world, people look different to each other. We want a Rwanda where people forget their ethnic differences. No Hutus and Tutsis, just Rwandans. My parents were driven out of Rwanda in 1959 because of such hatred. I grew up a refugee because of such hatred. Do you, Fergal, really think I want to go back and impose some new kind of tribalism on Rwanda? No way, my friend, there is no way I want that.' This was more than a prepared speech. I knew from the passion in his voice, the slight edge of impatience with my question that Frank believed in what he was saying. This was a conviction informed by hard remembrance. Frank Ndore had grown up in a foreign country and had learned his military skills in the National Resistance Army of Yoweri Museveni. In Frank's mind tribalism had robbed him of a country he could call his own. He might still have been fighting on the front line but his easy manner and good communications skills had come to the personal attention of the RPF's commander-in-chief, General Paul Kagame. He had singled Frank out to be one of the main battlefield guides for the groups of foreign journalists who had started arriving in Rwanda in the previous weeks. Somewhere along the line Frank had picked Valence out from the ranks of young soldiers to be his bodyguard. Now they were a team.

Once we were inside the car, Frank in the lead vehicle with David, Moses and myself, and Valence in the second car with the others, I asked about Valence.

'Where did he come from, Frank? He has no English so he can't have grown up in Uganda.'

'No, man,' he replied, 'he's from the south of Rwanda. He joined us back in '92 when the pogroms were going on against the Tutsis. He has a sad story. At the start of the killing a few weeks back the Interahamwe came to his family home. They killed nearly all of his family. I am not sure how many but his mother and father and some brothers and sisters. There are two sisters alive and he is looking for them, but we are not sure where they are. There is no point in asking him about what happened because he does not talk about it, except very rarely to me. He is wanting to put it behind him and be a good soldier.'

I looked back and saw Valence smiling and gesticulating with his hands as Tony and Glenn kept up their attempts at conversation. The boy soldier Valence, proud and neat, was the other half of the RPF equation, part of the new generation of Tutsi refugees. There was an important difference, though. Valence was not leaving for another country. His people might have been butchered but the RPF had given him the wherewithal to stay and fight. Perhaps it would be too strong to say that Frank took a fatherly interest in Valence, but he could easily have chosen a tougher, more experienced bodyguard. I think he saw something of his younger self in the boy and it was this he reached out to protect in the midst of chaos and war.

CHAPTER THREE

Orphans

North of Byumba, and we are dipping into a long valley. The countryside is a sheet of deep green that rises in terraces on either side of the road. There are fields full of banana, and avocado plantations. The fruit sits on the trees ripening in the still heat of the late afternoon. Birds drop occasionally into the trees and peck at the green bananas. They feast until they are hardly able to fly because there are no humans to scare them away. There is a silence here that is more than the absence of noise. This is the quiet of death and abandonment. We pass empty cabin after cabin. Outside most of the buildings are scattered pots and pans and broken furniture, the scraps of clothing that the occupants could not carry when they fled. The cabins are built from mud with roofs of thatch or corrugated iron. A family dog sits gazing down the road in the direction his owners must have taken when they fled. We slow down and wave to the dog, which rises slowly from its haunches and begins to growl. 'It's not an RPF dog,' jokes Frank. The people of this area were Hutus who fled before the advancing rebel armies in the previous few weeks.

Before that at least some of them had joined the slaughter of their Tutsi neighbours. Some of the houses here belong to Tutsis who will never come back to reclaim them. An occasional cow wanders into the middle of the road and Moses must swerve to avoid a crash.

It is four hours since we left Mulindi and the journey through the emptiness, which at first disturbed us, is now becoming tedious. We are tired and hot and thirsty and I at least am starting to feel sorry for myself. Then to our left we see a lake and beside it is camped a group of maybe twenty or thirty people. 'They are Tutsis,' explains Frank, 'they have been rescued by our troops and they are looking for their way home.' The refugees are sitting by the water's edge and seem drained of life. The men are carrying large clubs and bows and arrows. The women are clustered around a small fire and boiling a pot of water. There is stillness and quiet except for the crying of several small, hungry children who are wandering around amid the piles of belongings on the ground. These 'belongings' consist of perhaps six large baskets into which have been crammed blankets, a few blackened pots and some vegetable roots and rice. As we pass, the people look up nervously. The sight of Frank's RPF uniform reassures them and they wave.

Nobody knows how many people are on the move in Rwanda in these chaotic days of early June. In the south nearly a million Hutus are supposed to be heading in the direction of the Zairean border as the RPF closes around Kigali and Gitarama. Quarter of a million more have crossed into Tanzania in the east. The Tutsis who have survived the killing are moving into rebel-held territory from hide-outs all over the country. Even as we travel there are searches going on all over the government area for Tutsis. The group we have just passed are lucky. From the stories emerging from the government-held areas, we know that most Tutsis don't make it past the first roadblock. David asks Frank how the rebels cater for the Tutsi refugees. 'They try and get to where our camps are and we do what we can, but we don't have food to feed an entire population. They do the best they can with what they find,' he explains. I think of a story I had been told a few days earlier in Nairobi by Joao Da Silva, a South African photographer. He had just come out of government-held territory, a long frightening journey through endless roadblocks manned by drunk militiamen and increasingly twitchy soldiers. Along the way he had stopped at a Catholic mission run by some Spanish nuns. By the time Joao arrived at the mission there were only two nuns left. The Hutu sisters had fled, the Tutsis had been abducted by the militia. One of the Spanish nuns was an old woman, around eighty years of age. The other, he guessed, was in her forties. The nuns seemed very frightened. When Joao asked what was wrong they led him to a small room at the rear of the convent. As they approached there was a short scuffling noise inside the room. The old nun opened the door and when Joao looked inside he saw that the room was full of Tutsi orphans. The sound of feet approaching down the pathway had led to a momentary panic inside the room. These were the children of murdered parents and now they were in hiding for their own lives. The old nun and her colleague had decided they could not abandon the children to their fate. Every other day the militia

*came to the mission and asked if they were hiding Tutsis. The
old nun faced them and said no, again and again. Any day now
she thought the militia would refuse to believe her and they
would search. And after that . . . well everybody knew what
would happen after that.*

The town of Byumba had been one of the first in the
country to fall to the rebels when they launched their
offensive in the days following the assassination of the
president. Because a lot of fighting had taken place in the
area since the first RPF invasion of 1990, Byumba was a
particular hotbed of Hutu extremism. There had been
training of Interahamwe groups here for more than three
years. But because the rebels moved quickly into the area,
the militias were not able to complete their task of eliminat-
ing the entire Tutsi population and the moderate Hutus who
opposed their agenda. As soon as the first rebel troops
began to appear outside the town the government forces
and their militia accomplices fled southwards.

We arrived in Byumba in the late afternoon, passing
through a succession of checkpoints manned by young
rebel soldiers. Many of them seemed to know Frank, and
they smiled when he rolled down the window and presented our ID cards for inspection. The town was almost
completely empty. An occasional civilian would drift across
the street but the houses and shops and offices were devoid
of a living presence. We scouted for an empty building in
which to make camp. Eventually Frank signalled to a fine

villa and we clambered out, forcing open the gate and
wandering inside. Frank told us that a government civil
servant had lived here. Now the RPF had requisitioned
the house for the use of passing officers and guests. There
was a table and four chairs and three beds but everything
else had been taken away. Glenn and Tony began what
was to become our nightly ritual of making camp: starting
up the generator that gave us light and a reassuring buzz of
noise, hoisting mosquito nets into the air and arranging our
sleeping-bags close together, so that if one of us should
wake in the dark and silence of the Rwandan night, there
would be the comforting presence of other figures near by.

I was nominated cook and began to prepare our food: a
menu of tinned meat and beans and rice bought in the
markets of Kampala. As the first odours of cooked food
began to rise from the Primus stove, I noticed that more
and more people, some of them soldiers, others refugees,
were beginning to assemble in the garden of the villa. One
of the soldiers smiled at me and rubbed his stomach. 'Oh,
Christ, we're going to have to feed the whole bloody
town,' I groaned to Tony, who was sitting beside the
stove. 'Don't worry about it, man. They would give it to
us if they had it. Remember in Africa you share what you
have. This isn't like Europe or Jo'burg, where you hold on
to what you have just for yourself. You better get used to
it,' he replied. Tony did not intend his words to be a
rebuke but I felt ashamed and selfish. I felt like an alien. I
was operating on an idea of private property that would

have been entirely appropriate in London or New York, but not in the African bush in the middle of a civil war. 'You're right, Tony, man. I was just afraid we would run out of food later on down the road. No, we'll find something somewhere even if we do run out. I'm sorry,' I said, mentally subdividing the portions to include our ten or so unexpected guests.

We were just finishing dinner with our array of guests when David strode through the gates of the villa. I had been so busy dishing up food that I hadn't noticed his absence. He came straight over to where I was sitting with Tony and spoke briskly: 'All right, chaps, time to get a move on. There is something very interesting just outside the town.' Somewhere in the background I heard one of the drivers groan at the prospect of yet more movement. 'What is it? Can't it wait until the morning?' I asked. 'Orphans,' said David, 'a camp full of orphans on the other side of town. It won't take us ten minutes and we still have a good two hours' light. Come on, chaps, up and go.' And with that he had turned around and was marching out to the cars with a vigour and sense of purpose that roused everybody to action. At sixty David was nearly twice my age, yet he seemed to have more energy than the entire group of us put together. For twenty-five years he had been tramping around Africa, poking his aquiline nose into the doings of dictators and despots, badgering corrupt officials and wheedling his way into places most other journalists would never dream of going to. He had produced a brilliant film and book on the Afrikaners, *The White Tribe of Africa*, and was married to a South African. David was profoundly disinclined to romanticizing about Africa, but he loved the continent and abhorred the ignorant value judgements that urged a policy of abandonment by the west. Perhaps more than anything I admired his old-fashioned journalistic honesty. David believed in going to places and finding out what was happening, talking to as many sides as possible, and only then making up his mind. In this he was different from many producers who arrived with their own predetermined ideas of what the story should be and then sought out the voices to support their theories. He wasn't a glamorous media figure, nor was he political in the sense of fighting internal battles within the BBC. Although it is hard to guess at the true motives of a colleague, I liked to think that David Harrison was moved ultimately by the oldest and most noble journalistic aspiration of all: to seek the truth and report it whatever the consequences. Certainly in Rwanda, as we journeyed out into the country, I sensed in him a growing anger and determination. The bad guys were really, really bad guys and David wanted to make sure as many people in the world knew who they were and what they did.

By the time we arrived at the orphanage the youngest children were already being bedded down for the evening. Now, as I write, I am still confronted by those small faces with their great wide eyes gazing up at me from beneath their blankets on the rough concrete floor. There were several hundred children here, of all ages up to late teens. They had lost their parents and other family members in the massacres of the previous weeks. The orphanage had until a few days previously been a luxury hotel to which Rwanda's Hutu elite had come to enjoy the panoramic views and clear air of the mountains outside Byumba. The building had been left intact, but the hotel owners had taken everything they could carry when they fled south. The new 'manager' of the hotel was a beautiful young woman named Rose Kayitesi. She welcomed Frank like a long-lost friend. Later he told us that she had been in the mountains with his unit in the early days of the guerrilla war. 'She was a good fighter against the government troops,' he said. But now, with thousands of orphaned children flooding into rebel territory, Rose had abandoned her military fatigues and set up a reception centre for the young refugees. Here they were clothed and fed and comforted by Rose and her team of volunteers until the RPF could find substitute parents from among those who had survived the genocide.

In what had once been the lobby of the hotel, there were about fifty children between the ages of six and eight. They were not wounded, although some coughed violently, the result of having had to sleep out in the wet fields to avoid the Interahamwe. I smiled at them and some of the children beamed back and giggled among themselves. 'They are not used to white visitors but they know that you are not here to harm them,' said Rose. 'We are trying to teach them to trust the world again, but it is very, very difficult.' We left the room and followed Rose down a stone staircase. At the end was a wide space of ground where the brightly coloured clothes of several hundred children had been laid out to dry. Beyond the clothing was a latrine pit that the RPF guards had dug. Squatting there in the dusk were two tiny girls who looked up at me and smiled with expressions of such aching sweetness that I faltered for a moment and had to turn my face away.

Rose led us to a circle of seats and asked us to sit down. Another worker was sent to gather a group of children for their evening wash. Buckets of water were produced and soap and towels. The smallest ones, infants of about three and four, were lined up first and scrubbed and dried. None of the children cried or complained. Then I saw a little girl crawling around on the ground near the steps. I think she must have been four or five years old. She made no sound at all but when she sat down she rocked back and forth incessantly. Nobody knew what had happened to her parents because she had not spoken since the day the RPF soldiers had found her wandering in the bush. Rose walked over and the child ceased her rocking and held out her arms so that she could be lifted into the comforting embrace. 'There are so many like her. So many who have lost their voices because of what they have seen,' explained Rose, as she gently patted the child's head.

A group of children gathered around us. Among them

was another girl whose head and right arm were heavily bandaged. I cannot remember her name but her story left me wordless. 'The Interahamwe came to our house and they asked all who are *inyenzi* (cockroaches) to step outside. They knew that we were Tutsis, these people, because some of them are our neighbours. When we did not come out they broke down the door. We were inside and could hear them shouting. And then they came through the front door and I followed my parents and brothers and sisters out into the fields at the back and we ran. But they ran fast and caught us and they killed my family members and they thought they had killed me too. They hit me with the machetes and clubs and then threw all the bodies together so that I was lying under my mother who was dead. But I was not dead and at night I crawled away and hid in the fields where the grass was very high. Then after a time the soldiers of the RPF came and they helped me and brought me here.' Now Rose was attempting to find a family who would take the child.

'We believe these children must stay in Rwanda. They are Rwandese children and we do not want them sent abroad to other countries.' As she spoke I could see Frank nodding furiously. There had been offers from foreigners to adopt some of the children but all had been politely declined. What would they do in a foreign country, far from their homeland with all their memories and nobody around them who really understood what had happened? There was, I suspected, another factor at work, one that

had a great deal to do with the refugee memories of the
RPF leadership. Having been made exiles themselves in
1959, they were not going to allow another generation of
Tutsi children to be forced out of their country. I stood to
one side while Glenn and Tony filmed the children sitting
with Rose. Frank came up and spoke quietly. 'You know
they wanted to kill all of the children. They were sorry
they had not killed all of our families back in 1959 so there
would have been nobody left to go abroad and form a
resistance. This time they wanted to finish the job . . . get
rid of the Tutsis once and for all.' This was not paranoia.
There were too many eyewitness accounts of children
being systematically targeted and killed. 'Don't repeat the
mistake of 1959' became the catch-phrase among the militias as they went from house to house seeking out Tutsis.
Children proved much easier quarry than adults. Most did
not have the resourcefulness, the knowledge of territory
and the survival skills of older people. Some clung to their
parents and were easily finished off. Others watched from
hiding places and screamed as they saw other members of
their families being murdered. The militias were always on
the alert for the exclamations of small frightened voices.
Once caught, children were much easier to kill. The little
body frames were clubbed and hacked down within minutes. Some, however, survived their appalling injuries.
There were many accounts of children who hid under
mounds of bodies until they felt it was safe to crawl
out. Rose said that many of the children called out

at night in their sleep. Some called for dead parents; others screamed out in the grip of some nightmare whose depth of terror even she, with her experience of war, could not begin to contemplate. For some children the destruction of their entire family groups had robbed them of the will to live. Frequently as we journeyed through Rwanda, we would hear of little boys and girls who had literally died of sorrow, withdrawing from everyone and refusing to eat or drink, until they finally wasted away.

A small boy came up to the circle. He was smiling brightly and tapping his left hand against his thigh. There was a large bandage around his head smeared with the rust of dried blood. Rose said that he had been struck in the head by a spear. The boy could no longer control his bowels and seemed to have lost his mind.

It was dark when we said goodbye to Rose and her children. David, who had been so full of vigour on the way to the orphanage, was quiet as we drove back to our billet. So too were Tony and Glenn and the two drivers. We had come to the end of our first day in Rwanda.

CHAPTER FOUR

Nyarubuye

Begin with the river. From where I stand near the bridge it looks like a great soup. It is brown with upland silt and thick with elephant grass. It has come swirling down from the far reaches of the land and is fat with rain. I am arguing with Frank. 'Marriage is for old men and idiots,' says Frank. 'You should try it first, you old cynic,' I tell him. Frank believes in loving and leaving, or so he says. I think he had some kind of special feeling for Rose but he won't admit it. I think his talk about having girlfriends everywhere is just a front. Frank is quiet and shy around women. There is an exaggerated politeness about him, even when he is with women soldiers of the RPF. 'How could I be married anyway doing this job?' he asks. Valence is standing behind us and polishing his rifle. Frank says something to him in Kinyarwanda and he laughs. 'What was that?' I ask. 'Oh, I just told him you were looking for a wife for me,' he replies and we both laugh. The talk goes on like this for several more minutes. It is pleasantly distracting. So much so that at first I do not notice them. And then I turn around and for the first time I see two bodies bobbing along. Then three more. They nudge in and out of the grass and the leaves and are carried towards the falls. One swirls in towards the bank and I notice that it is a woman who has been chopped and hacked. But it is not the gash in her head, the gouges in her back and arms, that frighten and offend. Rather, I am shocked by her nakedness. Like the others she is bloated and her bare body turns and drops and turns and drops in the current. Near the bridge the current picks up and I watch her tumble down into the white water, disappearing fast. She comes up again, head first, and is bounced against the rocks.

'Don't worry man. Don't be surprised,' says Frank. 'They've been coming through in their hundreds.' I look down directly on to the falls and see that there are two bodies wedged tight into the rocks. One is that of a man wearing a pair of shorts. He appears to be white, but this is because the days in the water have changed his colour. Near by there is a baby, but I can only make out the head and an arm. The infant is tossed around by the falling water but is tangled in the weeds that cover the lower part of the rocks. The force of the water is unable to dislodge the baby and so it bounces up and down in the foam. At this I turn and walk away from the bridge and quietly take my place in the back of the car.

The aKagera River flows from the highlands of Rwanda, down through the country until it crosses the border into Tanzania and then Uganda, finally filtering out into the vastness of Lake Victoria. The river therefore became an ideal carriageway for the dispersal of evidence of Rwanda's genocide. People were routinely lined up beside the river for execution and then pushed into the flood. An alternative method of killing was to force people to jump into the fast running water. Most drowned within a few minutes. The Interahamwe gangs noted that this was a particularly efficient way of killing small children, who were more easily carried off in the current. The exhortations of the extremist leaders (as noted in the Prologue) to send the Tutsis 'back to the Ethiopia' were coming home with a terrible vengeance. Many of the illiterate peasants who were roused to acts of murder believed that the aKagera did actually flow to Ethiopia. But almost every other river and lake in the country also became dumping grounds for the dead. There were so many bodies it seemed the earth could not hold them. When the dead finally reached Lake Victoria, Ugandan fishermen went out in their boats to recover them and give them a decent burial. Moses and Edward had heard of many men going out day after day without being paid, to gather in the corpses. Colleagues had seen the bodies of mothers and children who had been tied together and thrown into the water. There were thousands of corpses.

Driving down to the river, deeper into the heart of the killing grounds, I began to notice the first odours of death. As we drove along the road, the presence of corpses would be announced from a long distance, the rank smells reaching into the interior of our vehicles. I looked back and caught Glenn's eye. He shook his head and then buried his face in a small towel. But we could not see any dead people. They were lying out of view in the plantations and the storm drains, covered now by the thickly spreading vegetation of the summer. In this part of the country close to the border with Tanzania, there was nothing left. There were no people, no cattle, no cats and dogs. The militias had swept through the hills destroying everything before them in a plague of knives and spears.

That morning, as we were leaving Byumba, Frank told us about a massacre that had taken place in the townland of Nyarubuye near the Tanzanian border. An estimated 3,000 Tutsis had taken refuge in and around the parish church. Frank said that a handful of people had survived and were being looked after at a small camp in the offices of the former local administration. 'We can get there by this afternoon, if you want to. The tar road is good as far as Rusomo Commune and then we have to leave and go into the bush.' The journey passed in quietness and we half slept for several hours, until Frank directed the Land Rovers off the main road and on to a rough bush track.

This was always going to be the hardest part, this remembrance of what lay ahead in the dusk on that night in early June. My dreams are the fruit of this journey down the dirt road to Nyarubuye. How do I write this, how do I do justice to what awaits at the end of this road? As simply as possible. This is not a subject for fine words. We bounce and jolt along the rutted track on an evening of soft, golden light. The air is sweet with the smell of warm savannah grass. Clouds of midges hover around the cars, dancing through the windows. Although I can sense the nervousness of everybody in the car, we are exhausted and hungry from the long day's travelling, and we are too tired to bother fighting off the insects. Moses shifts down into first gear as we face into a long climb. The wheels begin to lose their grip and they spin in the loose sand of the incline. 'Oh, shit,' mutters Moses. We climb out and begin to shove and push, but the car rolls back down the hill and we have to jump out of the way. The countryside is vastly different to the deep green hills around Byumba. From the top of the hill we can see a great expanse of yellow savannah grass, dotted here and there with thornbush and acacia. Glenn says it reminds him of home. He is right. This could be the bushveld around Louis Trichardt in the far Northern Transvaal. After about fifteen minutes of manoeuvring Moses eventually gets the car going again and we move off. Frank has become very quiet and he is fingering the stock of his assault rifle. After about another fifteen minutes we come to a straight stretch of track, wider than before and with a line of tall trees on either side. Up ahead is the façade of a church built from red sandstone. 'This is Nyarubuye,' says Frank. Moses begins to slow the car down and Glenn is preparing his camera to film. As we drive closer the front porch of the church comes into view. There is a white marble statue of Christ above the door with hands outstretched. Below it is a banner proclaiming the celebration of Easter, and below that there is the body of a man lying across the steps, his knees buckled underneath his body and his arms cast behind his head. Moses stops the car but he stays hunched over the wheel and I notice that he is looking down at his feet.

I get out and start to follow Frank across the open ground in front of the church. Weeds and summer grasses have begun to cover the gravel. Immediately in front of us is a set of classrooms and next to that a gateway leading into the garden of the church complex. As I walk towards the gate, I must make a detour to avoid the bodies of several people. There is a child who has been decapitated and there are three other corpses splayed on the ground. Closer to the gate Frank lifts a handkerchief to his nose because there is smell unlike anything I have ever experienced. I stop for a moment and pull out my own piece of cloth, pressing it to my face. Inside the gate the trail continues. The dead lie on either side of the pathway. A woman on her side, an expression of surprise on her face, her mouth open and a deep gash in her head. She is wearing a red cardigan and a blue dress but the clothes have begun to rot away, revealing the decaying body underneath. I must walk on, stepping over the corpse of a tall man who lies directly across the path, and, feeling the grass brush against my legs, I look down to my left and see a child who has been hacked almost into two pieces. The body is in a state of advanced decay and I cannot tell if it is a girl or a boy. I begin to pray to myself. 'Our Father who art in heaven . . .' These are prayers I have not said since my childhood but I need them now. We come to an area of wildly overgrown vegetation where there are many flies in the air. The smell is unbearable here. I feel my stomach heave and my throat is completely dry. And then in front of me I see a group of corpses. They are young and old, men and women, and they are gathered in front of the door of the church offices. How many are there? I think perhaps a hundred, but it is hard to tell. The bodies seem to be melting away. Such terrible faces. Horror, fear, pain, abandonment. I cannot think of prayers now. Here the dead have no dignity. They are twisted and turned into grotesque shapes, and the rains have left pools of stagnant, stinking water all around them. They must have fled here in a group, crowded in next to the doorway, an easy target for the machetes and the grenades. I look around at my colleagues and there are tears in Tony's eyes. Glenn is filming, but he stops every few seconds to cough. Frank and Valence have wandered away from us into a clump of trees and the older man is explaining something to the boy. I do not know what he is saying, but Valence is looking at him intensely. I stay close to David because at this moment I need his age and strength and wisdom. He is very calm, whispering into Glenn's ear from time to time with suggestions, and moving quietly. The dead are everywhere. We pass a classroom and inside a mother is lying in the corner surrounded by four children. The chalk marks from the last lesson in mathematics are still on the board. But the desks have been upturned by the killers. It looks as if the woman and her children had tried to hide underneath the desks. We pass around the corner and I step over the remains of a small boy. Again he has been decapitated. To my immediate left is a large room filled with bodies. There is blood, rust coloured now with the passing weeks, smeared on the walls. I do not know what else to say about the bodies because I have already seen too much. As we pass back across the open *ground in front of the church I notice Moses and Edward standing by the cars and I motion to them to switch on the headlights because it is growing dark. The sound of insects grows louder now filling in the churchyard silence. David and the crew have gone into the church and I follow them inside, passing a pile of bones and rags. There are other bodies between the pews and another pile of bones at the foot of the statue of the Virgin Mary. In a cloister, next to the holy water fountain, a man lies with his arms over his head. He must have died shielding himself from the machete blows. 'This is fucking unbelievable,' whispers Tony into my ear. We are all whispering, as if somehow we might wake the dead with our voices. 'It is just fucking unbelievable. Can you imagine what these poor bastards went through?' he continues. And I answer that no, I cannot imagine it because my powers of visualization cannot possibly encompass the magnitude of the terror. David and Glenn say nothing at all and Frank has also lapsed into silence. Valence has gone to join the drivers. I do not know the things Valence has seen before this and he will not talk about them. I imagine that the sight of these bodies is bringing back unwelcome memories. Outside the church the night has come down thick and heavy. Tony shines a camera light to guide our way. Even with this and the car lights I nearly trip on the corpse of a woman that is lying in the grass. Moths are dancing around the lights as I reach the sanctuary of the car. While we are waiting for Glenn and Tony to pack the equipment away, we hear a noise coming from one of the rooms of the dead. I turn to Moses and Edward. 'What is that? Did you hear that?'*

I ask. Edward notices the edge of fear in my voice and strains his ear to listen. But there is no more sound. 'It is only rats, only rats,' says Moses. As we turn to go I look back and in the darkness see the form of the marble Christ gazing down on the dead. The rats scuttle in the classrooms again.

There was little talk on the way back to the main road. Tony produced one of our whisky bottles and we passed it around. I took several long draughts and lit a cigarette and noticed then that my hands were shaking. Frank watched the road ahead closely and told Moses to drive as quickly as he could. The men who had done the killing, the Interahamwe of Rusomo Commune and Nyarubuye itself, might have fled to Tanzania, but they crossed the border at night to stage guerrilla attacks and to kill any Tutsis who might have escaped the massacres. I should have felt fear at that moment but I had too much anger inside. After a long silence it was Moses who spoke. 'How can they do that to people, to children? Just how can they do it?' he asked. Nobody answered him and he said nothing else. The journey back to the main road seemed to last an eternity. All along the way I could think only of the churchyard and the dead lying there in the dark. Although the sight of the massacre made me feel ill, I was not frightened of the dead. They were not the source of evil that filled the air at Nyarubuye and that now began to undermine my belief in life. Now that we had left, the killing ground would be quiet again. Perhaps the militiamen passed there from time to time as they crossed back and forth into Tanzania. Were they still able to pass the scene of their crimes without feeling guilt? Did the rotting dead frighten them? The killers must have moved in close to their victims. Close enough to touch their shaking bodies and smell their fear. Were there faces among the crowd that they recognized? After all, the militiamen came from the same neighbourhood. Some of them must have been on speaking terms with the people who pleaded for mercy. I thought of Seamus Heaney's line about 'each neighbourly murder' in the backroads of County Fermanagh. Back in the North of Ireland I had reported on numerous cases of people being murdered by men who worked with them or who bought cattle and land from them. In Rwanda that intimate slaughter was multiplied by tens of thousands.

By the time we reached the main road again it was nearly midnight. We had been warned sternly against travelling late at night on Rwanda's roads, even inside areas that were controlled by rebel forces. The militia were one problem, nervous sentries sitting in some lonely outpost were another, potentially more dangerous one. Frank warned Moses to approach each checkpoint slowly with headlights dipped. He needn't have worried. Moses, veteran of Amin's Uganda, knew his way around military checkpoints and was punctiliously slow and precise when he pulled up to the blockades. The soldiers were less friendly at night. Even Frank with all his ease of manner could not puncture the atmosphere of sullen fear at the dark roadblocks.

We had passed the last roadblock before Rusomo Commune when the headlights picked out the figures of six or more people struggling wearily along the road. I called out to Moses to stop just ahead of them. As we pulled in to the roadside I noticed that the group, a woman, three men and two small children, had halted in their tracks. They stood looking from our car back to the Land Rover carrying Glenn and Tony. The men were tall and thin and carried bows and arrows. One clutched a large rooster under his arm. The creature's legs had been fastened together and its beak tied up. The woman held a baby in the cradle of her left arm and as I approached I saw that the child was sucking relentlessly at one of her withered breasts. The woman was covered in dust and her face was gaunt. She would not look directly at us but kept a stare fixed on the ground. Clinging to her legs was a small boy of around six. 'Who are you?' asked Frank. The woman began to speak but her words came in a soft foggy voice. We could only hear isolated snatches of the sentence. Frank came closer and spoke again. 'It is all right, my dear, we are not here to harm you. Please speak louder and tell us who you are.' She spoke again, this time in a voice that was still difficult to hear, but Frank standing close by was able to translate. The woman had come from the area of Nyarubuye with the two small children. They had been hiding in the fields for more than a month when the three men had found them. At first she had feared that the men were militia and that she and the children would be killed.

But one of the men, the one named Silas, was a neighbour and she knew him to be a Tutsi like herself. 'How did you survive?' asked Frank. 'We hid in the places of wild countryside and covered ourselves with grass and bushes and we ate roots and berries. We were eating grass like the cows. There were bodies everywhere dumped in the fields and ditches. It was hard and I thought we would starve to death. This would have happened if the men had not found us,' she replied. For four long weeks this woman and children had watched from their hiding place as the killers scoured the countryside around them. Not once did the baby or the small boy cry out. She did not know why this was except perhaps that the children must have had some inner sense of the danger. Throughout the conversation the small boy twisted and turned around the woman's legs. The man named Silas spoke up and said that the boy was not her child. His parents had been killed at Nyarubuye and he had escaped into the countryside. Somehow he had met up with the woman and her baby, and together the small group had evaded the militia bands who were hunting down survivors. The woman was alive because she had not gone to Nyarubuye with the other Tutsis. They had mistakenly believed that they would find sanctuary in the house of god. Some instinct had told her that the church was the least safe place to be. The woman's husband was gone, however. She would only say the word 'gone' as if unable to admit that he had joined the ranks of the dead. Although the woman seemed weary beyond words, the group was heading deeper into rebel-held territory, as far away from the border and the predatory bands of Interahamwe as they could go. Having survived once, she was not about to gamble with her life and those of the children. They said goodbye and began to walk slowly down the road. The little boy glanced backwards occasionally until we could see them no more.

That night we arrive at the Office of the Bourgmestre of Rusomo, Sylvestre Gacumbitsi. He has fled to Tanzania along with the Hutu population of the area. The building has several offices and also housed a health centre. There are piles of syringes and boxes of condoms. Thousands of condoms. On the floor in the main office is the Rwandan flag, the flag of the old regime. It is green, yellow and red with a large black R in the middle. Somebody has laid it across the floor so that it looks like a brightly coloured doormat. The building has sustained almost no war damage, and the rebels have not looted the stores of medical and office equipment. Most poignantly in a room at the very back is a library of index cards. These are in fact the identity cards of every local resident. There are thousands of these thin paper cards on to which are fixed the photographs of the bearers. Each card is marked with the name, address and ethnic identity of the resident, Hutu, Tutsi, Twa or other. Dust has gathered on the cards, and when I flick through it rises up and stings my eyes and nose. The colonial government introduced this system of population registration and their Rwandan Hutu successors entrenched it as a means of political control. I have seen cards like these before, back in the bad old apartheid days in South Africa. They used to call them passbooks — little books that dictated who you were and where you could live. These cards are similar but I know that they have been used as instruments of genocide. With the ethnic identity and address of every resident registered here at the commune building, the Interahamwe had a ready-made death list. I look at face after face of Tutsis and wonder if any are still alive. Anybody who imagines that the killing was an arbitrary and disorganized tribal bloodbath had better come here. I have no doubt that this is an index list for murder, prepared years in advance and held in readiness for the day when the Tutsis might need to be sorted out. In a room at the front there are two RPF women soldiers patiently typing out passes for refugees. Many have fled here from far away and want to get home. The RPF has set up a reception centre for Tutsi refugees, where there is at least physical security and some small amount of medical care.

As we prepare to bed down in one of the old offices, Frank comes in and motions to David and myself to follow him. 'There are some survivors here, some survivors of Nyarubuye.' His voice is unusually excited and we follow him to a small room from where the light of a candle flickers against the glass panes of the doorway. The room is tiny, perhaps big enough for two people. There are six patients lying on mattresses inside. There is a smell of disinfectant mixed with the bad smell of septic wounds. Of the six patients five are children. One little girl lies in the corner, her head and hands heavily bandaged. A nurse comes in to change her dressings and she cries out, not loudly, but with a soft whimpering sound. David kneels down and begins to comfort her. As the nurse peels off the bandage on her head the girl grits her teeth. Underneath is a deep, black gash. The wound is festering. Some adult hit this child on the head with a machete and when she raised her hands to ward off the blows he struck fingers because they too are mutilated and black. Her name is Varentina and she is not expected to survive the gangrene that has infected the wounds.

There are no pain killers here. Anything that might have been of use to the rebels was taken into Tanzania by the escaping Hutus. I go outside and fetch Tony, who is our medic on the journey. He brings Panadol, pitifully inadequate to stem the terrible pain, but it is all we have. The small white tablets are given to the nurse, who shares them out among the wounded. The older woman is complaining of a terrible pain in her head. She rocks back and forth, crying. The nurse pulls back her shawl and reveals a terrible deep wound to the skull. The woman rubs her hand against the wound and continues to cry. The other children are used to this because they pay more attention to us than to anything else that is taking place. David goes outside and comes back several minutes later with a bag full of sweets. He had bought these back in Kampala and in his fatherly way doled them out to us as lunch on our journey down from the border. Methodically and gently, he goes from child to child and hands out sweets. They do not grab the sweets but quietly place them in their mouths. The woman holds out her hand and thanks us and turns to the children and reminds them to say thank-you. She tells us that her name is Flora Mukampore, a Tutsi from the area of Nyarubuye. 'Come in the morning,' she says, 'come in the morning and I will tell you the story of what happened to us there.'

They had heard the news about the president's plane from some Tutsi neighbours who had heard the story on the radio. Everybody knew it would be bad. The militias had been training in the area for a long time, months and months. The Tutsis knew about lists of people that were going around, lists of Tutsis who were to be killed. These names were being circulated among the Interahamwe and the police for weeks ahead of the plane crash. The killing started soon after the crash on 6 April. Gangs of militia were going through the hills with whistles. They blew on the whistles to make the Tutsis come out of their homes. Many of these men were drunk and they had a look of madness in their eyes. They set fire to the huts of the Tutsis and took their cattle. It was death for any Tutsi who was in their way. The closer the gangs got to Nyarubuye the more frightened the Tutsis became. Some of their Hutu neighbours were kind and offered to help them. But they were threatened by others who promised to tell the Interahamwe that they were helping the Inyenzi. It was worst at night. There was screaming and shooting and people were waiting to die. The Tutsis decided to form a deputation and they went to Rusomo to see the Bourgmestre, Sylvestre Gacumbitsi. He was a big man in the area, a member of President Habyarimana's MRND, and he had power with the police and army. Without his help the Tutsis knew that it was only a matter of time before they were all killed. Some of the Tutsis did business with Gacumbitsi. Somebody said his personal driver was a Tutsi. They believed that only the Bourgmestre could save them now. But when they went to see him, he turned them away. Gacumbitsi would not give them protection. He told them to go to the church and try to find safety there. The people were shocked by this and they believed they would definitely be killed unless they defended themselves. The word spread quickly and thousands of Tutsis from the surrounding area fled to the church at Nyarubuye. People came with their children and their livestock and whatever they could carry. Flora Mukampore had gone with her husband's family. The priests and the sisters were kind but more and more people kept coming and there was very little space. The men had bows and arrows and spears. Some of the boys gathered as many stones as they could. People set up camp and waited. Many went into the church and prayed for deliverance. It was not long before the militia arrived at the church and began to attack the refugees. People screamed and there was panic among the children. But the men and boys were able to drive them away with their home-made weapons. The militia retreated but as they left the men could hear them swearing that they would return. There was no way out of Nyarubuye now. All of the roads and the mountain tracks were crawling with Interahamwe. The militia returned some days later. This time they had the army and police with their guns and grenades.

Flora noticed that the leader of group was none other than Sylvestre Gacumbitsi. In his car there were several policemen and a whole pile of machetes. She saw Gacumbitsi hand out the weapons. After that there was chaos. The soldiers moved in first and began to shoot; the bows and arrows were no use against guns. People were running everywhere. After the first lot of killing the militias went through finishing people off with machetes. Flora saw Gacumbitsi giving them their orders. A militiaman attacked her. She thought she recognized his face and she begged for mercy. But he just shouted at her and brought the machete down on her head. Flora collapsed and felt more bodies falling on top of her. All day the military, the police and the Interahamwe were chasing people around and killing them. They hunted them down in rooms and in the fields around the church and inside the building itself. When they had killed everyone, or so they thought, Gacumbitsi's gang left. But underneath the mounds of corpses lay survivors, including Flora. For a week and a half she hid under the bodies, venturing out at night to try and find water, and then returning to her grim hiding place for the day. She could not remember just how long it was before a small boy came and brought some RPF soldiers who took her to hospital. Now she had this endless pain in her head and she had dreams about the massacre all the time. Flora did not know where her family was and had no idea where she would go when her wounds healed. But of all things about the massacre what she cannot believe is that Gacumbitsi himself actually came and directed the killing of the people. He was their Bourgmestre and he had organized the killing. Even his refusing to help them she could understand. He might have been afraid himself. But to go and tell the others to kill people. This was something terrible.

As Flora was finishing her story, sitting in the bright morning sunshine outside the clinic, a man came up and sat beside her. I recognized Silas, one of the escorts we had met on the previous night returning from Nyarubuye. 'I was there too. I was at Nyarubuye,' he said. 'I hid in the thick bushes near by and saw the killing and I saw Gacumbitsi. He was giving out the weapons and telling his men to finish people off. He helped to finish some people off himself. I saw him.' Silas offered to take us to Gacumbitsi's house. It was on the road south, on the way to Tanzania. Perhaps we would find something there, maybe some photographs of the Bourgmestre or some documents. Barely half an hour later we were standing in the ransacked living-room of Sylvestre Gacumbitsi. Furniture and cloth-ing were strewn everywhere. Sticks of chalk had been spilled on the floor and now formed a fine white powder that rose up in little clouds when we walked. There were piles of old letters in French. All seemed to have been written by one of Gacumbitsi's children to friends at school. The content was mundane. 'How are you these days? I am very well. I am studying hard . . .' Above the fireplace was a citation from Pope John Paul II. It was the routine blessing of the house usually purchased as a gift in Rome and familiar to most Catholics. Close by was a sacred heart lamp and near that some photographs of the Bourgmestre. Gacumbitsi was a big man, tall and broad with a closely trimmed beard and handsome, confident face. In one of the photographs he is seen as a devoted family man, one baby in his arms, and his wife and three other children standing beside him. In another he is standing next to a cow that is apparently being presented to him by another man. There was something unusual about this photograph. The man who is giving the cow looks dejected, as if he wanted to be anywhere but in this picture. Silas explained that the man was a Tutsi he knew. He thought the man was probably dead by now. On Gacumbitsi's orders they had lined people up along the roadway and killed them, and Silas thought this man might have been caught trying to escape. In the courtyard of the house we found a communion chalice, looted presumably at Nyarubuye. Near by was Gacumbitsi's party membership card. The heat had melted the laminated plastic but the writing was still legible. The card had been given to the Bourgmestre to allow him to attend the last major party conference the previous year. There he would have heard the late President Habyarimana rail against the RPF and pledge resistance to power-sharing with them. Beyond the high green hedge that surrounded the house were Gacumbitsi's plantations, heavy now with the smell of avocados, bananas and coffee. The plantations stretched over several acres and suggested that the Bourgmestre was a very prosperous man. In a few weeks it would be time to harvest the avocados. But the owner had fled and his labourers were either refugees or dead. The harvest would simply rot away. Walking back to the roadway, David spoke up: 'Why don't we see if we can go into Tanzania and track him down? Wouldn't that be something, to find him?' He spoke with his usual enthusiasm but my immediate reaction was one of scepticism. 'You're talking about going into a refugee camp with at least quarter of a million people from all over Rwanda and trying to find one man. Plus that refugee camp will be crawling with his supporters, all of whom have killed people . . . I'll give it a try but I don't fancy our chances,' I said. 'Well, if you're game, I am, and we can only try,' came the reply. I looked at Glenn and Tony and the two drivers. I cannot be absolutely sure, but I think all of them smiled. By now we knew, and trusted, David well enough to take the chance. A few minutes later we drove down the road towards the border with Tanzania in search of Sylvestre Gacumbitsi.

CHAPTER FIVE

A Servant of the People

The smoke from the fires of Benaco found us long before we saw the camp. I suddenly found myself rubbing my eyes and beginning to cough as the fumes from unseen fires filled the air. On either side of the roadway the countryside had been stripped bare of vegetation. Only the yellow savannah grass remained and the stumps of trees that had been hacked down as the waves of refugees moved across the land in search of a safe haven inside Tanzania. Some 250,000 people were known to have travelled down this road in a single day. Many thousands more had come in the weeks since the president's plane had crashed. Most were Hutus fleeing the advancing army of the RPF, but there were scattered groups of Tutsis, some of them posing as Hutus in order to save their lives. Already stories were filtering out of the camps about the murders of Tutsis who had been exposed by their neighbours. The UN and the international aid agencies had established a series of camps around the area of Ngara, and it was here that Sylvestre Gacumbitsi and numerous others accused of complicity in the genocide had found sanctuary. They were being housed and fed by the international community and were allowed, according to every eyewitness report, to organize their people as they saw fit within the confines of the camps. We had heard from several sources that Gacumbitsi was somewhere in the system of camps, but nobody knew precisely where.

As we came closer and closer, the air thickened and became foggy. Long lines of women and children filed along the roadway. The women carried piles of firewood stacked high on their heads. Beside them children struggled with branches and twigs that scratched along the ground, causing trails of dust to rise up behind them. I rolled down the window and heard a growing murmur of voices. It swelled as we drove to the top of the hill, until the sound resembled a great swarm of bees, into which had been mixed the noise of car horns and growling lorries. At the top of the hill we pulled in to the side of the road and I found myself looking down on the UN refugee camp at Benaco, the latest receptacle for the displaced of Rwanda. From the hillside the camp spread out before us in the dusk like a ragged flag. There were patches of white where the UN had erected feeding stations, innumerable squares of blue where plastic huts had been erected, and moving between and around them a great mass of brown figures. From my vantage point on the roadway the camp seemed to be a place of incessant movement. In the middle there was a main pathway, along which thousands of people were moving up and down in an orderly line. As we drove down a track towards the UN main compound I noticed that the crowds were moving to and from a lake. They carried water in buckets, pails, plastic bags, anything that could be filled.

I had never seen so many people crowded into one place. The air was by now thick with smoke; my lungs began to heave, and I coughed constantly. Down in the heart of the camp, the noise that had seemed a murmur from afar had become a loud, declamatory roll that rose above the refugees and hung in the air with the smoke and the smell of displaced people. Until a few weeks ago these people had lived and worked in Rwanda. They were farmers, businessmen, teachers – an entire society transplanted on to Tanzanian soil. We followed the crowds down to the shores of the lake. As we came closer, the crowds thickened and voices shouted and argued. The people were heading in the direction of a pump, from which the nightly water supply for cooking and cleaning was being distributed. I got out of the car and followed Tony and Glenn into the crowds. People pressed in around us and we began to slip on the mud. There were children scrambling to hold on to the hands of their parents and other, older ones who weaved in and around the adults. The people were completely indifferent to our presence. The camp had been a focus of media attention for several weeks now, and the refugees had become accustomed to the presence of camera crews. There were fierce arguments among the refugees as they pushed to get to the pump. I saw a man punch the man ahead of him in the queue. They began to jostle and slide on the mud until another, powerfully built refugee struck them both on the shoulders with a stick. They stopped fighting and scowled at the man who had intervened. Mingling with the woodsmoke was the nauseating smell of overcrowding: sweat, excrement, smoke and damp clothes. The people at Benaco were in a state of wretched poverty dependent on food hand-outs from the international community. They lived in plastic huts without sanitation, having lost their homes and land. Yet, as I moved among them, witnessing the squalor and desolation, I could not shut out the memory of Nyarabuye or the knowledge that among these huge crowds were thousands of people who had taken part in the genocide.

That night, after we had found space in a UN tent, David slipped out on his own, taking with him a young Hutu who had once worked for a western news agency in Kigali and who now found himself begging for food from the journalists who came through the camp. As the time slipped by, we began to worry. 'Where do you think he is?' I asked Glenn. 'Agh, man, you know what he's like. He's out there tormenting people into giving him Gacumbitsi's home address and telephone number,' he replied, and we laughed at the improbability of being able to find one man among more than quarter of a million. The truth

was that we did not even know for certain if Gacumbitsi
was in Benaco or whether he had gone deeper into Tanzania. Unlike the wretched mass outside our tent, Gacumbitsi
had money and probably transport. He would have had
the means to escape if he wanted to. By now Gacumbitsi
would have known that the RPF had taken over most of
Rwanda, and that his name would be high on their wanted
list. Staying in a camp so close to the border seemed to
represent his least likely option. Then Moses spoke: 'You
don't understand. He will want to be with his supporters.
He is not from Tanzania and without his supporters he is
nothing here. Even with money that will make no difference. He will have no power if he is not with his people.
That is why he is here somewhere.' Edward nodded his
agreement. 'In Africa a big man like that doesn't want to
be on his own running away. What will happen to his
power over the people while he is away? Someone else
will come in and the people will call him a coward. Moses
is right. Gacumbitsi is here and maybe very close.'

Later, as we prepared to bed down for the night, David
returned. He had found no definite news of Gacumbitsi,
but somebody had told him there was a sector of Benaco
where the refugees from Rusomo had set up camp. David
had a sense from those he had asked that Gacumbitsi was
there. He could not be sure, but he had an intuition. As we
drifted off to sleep amid the smells and noises of the camp,
David sat up and addressed us: 'We are going to find him,
chaps. We are going to find him.' And then, as was his

habit, he turned over and fell fast asleep, while I lay awake and worried about the day that lay ahead.

In the morning there is a cold wind coming in from the northeast. Dust and scraps of paper are blowing through the camp. The wind is carrying the smell of excrement and smoke away from us, and for the first time in days I breathe in clean air. The people who are living around us are friendly. They smile as we pass and their children come to the opening of the tent and gaze in, fascinated by the camera and the jumble of wires and batteries and plugs. I am feeling queasy this morning. The prospect of going out into the camp to search for a mass murderer fills me with apprehension. This is Hutu extremist territory and if anything goes wrong there will be no guns to protect us. The aid agencies are themselves scared of the militias who have begun to turn Benaco into a mini-Rwanda. I am bloody glad Glenn and Tony are here. I know from the South African townships that they are good men in a tight spot. Edward has volunteered to be the driver. Moses will stay with our equipment. 'If we find where he is, just stay in the car and keep the engine running in case we have to make a break for it,' I tell him. He seems excited by the prospect of the search. Moses, by contrast, looks weary and I am happy to let him rest in the tent. David has a piece of paper on which have been scribbled directions for the sector occupied by the Rusomo refugees. We head off into the camp and in no time we are lost. An Irish aid worker drives by and I flag her down. It is good to hear a voice from home, but she has no idea of where to look. For the next hour we go from one area to the next. In many areas there are men sharpening machetes and they look at us with an air of suspicion and hostility. One group is gathered around a radio. 'Beware of the cockroaches,' the presenter says. 'It is the duty of all Muhutu to rise up and resist the invasion of the cockroaches. Remember the victory of 1959. Let Rwanda not be destroyed by the invaders.' The voice crackles its poison into the minds of the loitering crowd. I am heartened by David's courage, however. He goes from group to group asking for directions. Eventually he strikes lucky. Somebody points him in the direction of the Rusomo refugees. 'About five minutes' drive away,' the man says. We find our way easily enough to the administrative centre that has been set up by the refugee leaders. 'Vous connaissez Monsieur Gacumbitsi, le Bourgmestre du Rusomo,' I say to the man at the door of the tent. My French is poor, augmented by David, who is standing right behind me while Glenn films the exchange. To our surprise the man is not hostile and offers to take us to Gacumbitsi's tent. Everything is remarkably calm, but I wonder how long it will be before somebody realizes we have come to ask Gacumbitsi some hard questions. The man who is our guide has great respect for Gacumbitsi. He tells us that the Bourgmestre is in charge of distributing food to the people from Rusomo. He is their leader inside the camp and he works with the UN to make sure that the people have everything they need. Our guide was studying to be a Catholic priest but because of the trouble he is now a refugee. He wants to go back to Rwanda but he is afraid of the RPF and thinks they will kill him. I want to ask him what he thinks of the genocide but it is too early. I need his confidence. I need him to believe that I am a friend. Not once does he ask us why we want to see Gacumbitsi. I think he is overawed by the equipment and by the fact of our 'whiteness'. There is something profoundly deferential in his attitude. How long will this last? I ask myself repeatedly. After about five minutes' driving we pull off the main track. 'From here we walk,' the guide says. I remind Edward to keep the engine running. As we walk deeper into a labyrinth of tents I start to wonder if the guide really is being deferential, or if is he luring us into a trap. We come to a hut made of branches and blue plastic. 'This is the hut of the Bourgmestre,' says the guide. Inside there are two women, a small girl and a teenager. These are the people whose empty, ransacked house I had visited two days earlier. The elder woman is suspicious. 'What do they want?' she asks. 'They simply want to talk to the Bourgmestre,' the guide replies. 'He is not here. Go to the UN offices. You will find him there,' she says, before closing the doorflap and ending the exchange. Now we know for certain that he is here somewhere and knowing this we cannot walk away.

When we get to the UN administrative offices there are more suspicious glances, this time from some of the employees of the UN who wonder what we are up to. Here the trail seems to run dry. Nobody seems to know where the Bourgmestre has gone. I start to worry that he has gone back home, we have missed him on the road. If that has happened then he will be warned by his wife and he may disappear. If a man wanted to lose himself in this camp it would be very easy. There would be no way of finding him. And then two men walk in and our guide's face lights up. 'They will know, they work with him,' he says.

There is a short conversation and the men point in the direction of a line of white tents and a stockade where the main grain supplies are being held.

Five minutes later I am walking with Glenn, Tony and David through a crowd of young Hutus who are standing outside the grain depot. Many of them are carrying machetes and they breathe hostility. I feel countless pairs of eyes following me as we turn a corner into the main loading area and see, standing with a group of older men, a face familiar from a photograph: the Bourgmestre of Rusomo, Sylvestre Gacumbitsi. 'It's now or never,' says Glenn, as we approach the group. I take the lead and Glenn comes in by my left shoulder, filming as we walk. David is on my right side. I can feel him breathing hard as we walk up to the group. 'Are you Sylvestre Gacumbitsi, the Bourgmestre of Rusomo?' I ask. David translates quickly into fluent French and Gacumbitsi nods. This is strange. He is smiling. He looks bemused. The men around him stand back. Some of them are carrying walkie-talkies. My heart is leaping against the wall of my chest and my face is twitching. I hope he does not sense my nervousness. That will give him courage to deny accusations or it may even prompt him to attack us. I decide to build up slowly. If I mention Nyarubuye immediately he may just walk off. Better to come gradually to the point and then hit him with the question as hard as I can. I ask about the conditions of the refugees and their food supplies and he answers. This man is big. The photograph didn't give the full impression of his size. He is at least six feet and broad-shouldered with a fat belly. He has a face that must have been handsome once but has now filled out to give him an air of smugness, arrogance. There are tribal scar marks on his cheeks. His beard is neatly trimmed and his slacks and blue striped shirt are spotlessly clean. Gacumbitsi stands out from the wretched peasantry who are lining up around the food compound. His personal bodyguards are also well dressed, but they are thin and wiry, and lack his air of assurance and command. Standing directly in front of him, I feel bloody small. I am perhaps five foot nine and fairly stocky. But there is something more than his physical size at work here. I know what this man is capable of. I remember the words of Flora and Silas and I have no reason to disbelieve them. Gacumbitsi, however, answers my initial questions politely. I know that he suspects us but he has decided to play the game coolly. He says something in Kinyarwanda to one of his henchmen and the man smiles back. What the hell was that, I say to myself. As he finishes speaking about the food distribution, I hit him with the first hard question.

'Mr Gacumbitsi, I want to ask what you know about the massacre at Nyarubuye?'

'I know nothing about any such event. Nothing.' He looks around him at the other men. But his face remains confident.

'Well, there are people who survived the massacre who say you do know about it,' I counter.

'No, I know nothing about that thing. It had nothing to do with me.'

This last sentence he utters with force and a slight hint of anger. Glenn is circling to keep the big man in frame. I catch Tony's eye and he nods his head in the direction of a group of

*youths who are looking at us with particular hostility. I am
silently communicating to him to keep an eye on them.*

'Mr Bourgmestre, I have spoken to eyewitnesses and survivors
and they all say you were there and that you organized the
killings. They also say you helped to finish people off who were
dying.'

He shakes his head. 'No, no, no . . . I am the Bourgmestre of
the Commune. Why would I do that? Why would I do that?
This thing had nothing to do with me. Who are these people
who say this against me?'

He is starting to seem less composed. I can tell he is struggling
to keep the anger from boiling up. It then occurs to me that he
may not have known before now that there were survivors.
Perhaps Gacumbitsi thought the militia had done for everyone.

'I have talked to the survivors, the Tutsis who survived the
killing at Nyarubuye.'

He stops and takes a step backwards and gives a mocking
laugh. 'Ah, I see. The Tutsis. The Tutsis.' There is real
venom in his voice. 'The Tutsis. What would you expect them
to say? I am a Hutu. They hate me. What would you expect
them to say except to blame me?' Gacumbitsi looks around into
the faces of his henchmen and nods his head. He smiles and they
smile. 'Let me tell you, my conscience is clear. I had nothing to
do with that episode,' he repeats.

When someone starts to deny like this, you have to push
harder. Everything I have heard and everything I sense about
Gacumbitsi tells me he is a killer. Hard words, an aggress-
ive approach are justified. 'Your conscience may be clear, Mr

Gacumbitsi, but there are a great many people who say your hands are bloody.'

He moves backwards again. This is becoming like a sparring match. 'Bring those people here who accuse me. Let them say it to my face. I repeat to you. I am innocent of these charges. I am the Bourgmestre of Rusomo. My job is to take care of the people. I did not kill people.'

The anger is starting to become obvious to his supporters and they stir among themselves. Glenn swings the camera around and attempts to photograph the young men with the machetes. They cover their faces. Gacumbitsi is tired of my questions and he returns to his men. The big man is carrying a clipboard and is in the process of organizing the distribution of rice. He is good at giving orders. A natural organizer. The men jump to his commands and outside the queues of people awaiting food are among the most orderly we have seen in the camp. Glenn and Tony follow him outside and, to our amazement, he agrees to be filmed organizing the food hand-outs. Perhaps he thinks this will reflect well on him, mitigate the harshness of the allegations. Perhaps he simply couldn't care less. There are foreign relief officials moving around the compound as well. I stop an American, a former Marine who comes from Texas and who is liaising with the Rwandans. 'Do you know that man is accused of mass murder? That man who is organizing the food distribution?' I ask. 'No, sir, I don't. We do not inquire into the background of every person who helps here. We leave it to the community to nominate who they want to work with us.'

And then I realize something I should have understood from our very first step into the camp. It is not the aid agencies or the UN or the Tanzanian government who are in control here. No, this vast city of huts and tents is the province of the Hutu warlords. Gacumbitsi is king here. He could have us beaten up, thrown out, even killed. But he is too clever for that. That might force the agencies or the Tanzanians to act as if they did have some control, and that would interfere with the system of power and patronage he has managed to transplant successfully from Rwanda to Benaco. Instead he has decided to tolerate us, humour us. He might suffer the indignity of being questioned and accused, but he knows what everybody knows. Nobody is going to come into his stronghold and take him away. It is because he has that knowledge that my questions are an irritant, little else. I think of Flora and Silas, and the little girl with her rotting head wound in the clinic at Rusomo, and the mounds of dead at Nyarubuye and the terror they must have felt as the killers closed in. I think of the unarmed and helpless dying under the bullets and knives of the militia. And then I look at Gacumbitsi, strutting among the refugees like a prince, a man whose power and influence has been guaranteed and protected by the governments of the world. I feel sick to my stomach. Just before we leave, the man who has been our guide tells me that the stories about massacres are all RPF propaganda. It was they who had killed the Tutsis just to blame the Hutus and take over the country. I thank him for his help and walk away.

★

The story of the refugee camps dominated the world news for much of May, June and July. The plight of the displaced Hutus became the focus of attention and the genocide a side issue. Riding on the back of international concern, the coterie of butchers who had organized and taken part in the slaughter of the Tutsis and moderate Hutus was able to find security in Tanzania and Zaire. The family and in-laws of President Habyarimana found safety in France, among them many of those who had been involved in the infamous Zero Network – the secret extremist group that had widespread support in the army and among the leaders of the Interahamwe. Men like Gacumbitsi were able to count on the ignorance and indifference of the international community. The simple truth was that nobody cared enough about the genocide to even think about going into the camps and arresting the warlords. I do not accept the argument that arrests would have led to a bloodbath. The armies of the west in particular have no lack of special forces units trained in abduction and kidnapping. This was not Somalia, where the Americans ran up against a well-armed opposition with a long tradition of guerrilla warfare. The Interahamwe, as they had proved when faced by the RPF, were by and large cowards who fled the moment they were confronted by superior firepower. In the camps at Benaco they were armed with machetes and axes. A few contingents of well-trained and armed troops would easily have disarmed them. The aid workers on the ground are not to be blamed for working with the likes of Gacumbitsi.

They were left in a pitifully exposed position by the UN and worked bravely under enormous pressures. When the Tanzanians attempted to crack down on the warlords, the aid workers found themselves surrounded by angry mobs threatening to kill them. It was at that point that a decisive show of force could have changed the situation. Because Rwanda's genocide was an affair of mass complicity into which tens of thousands of ordinary Hutus were drawn, there were difficult choices to make about who constituted a reasonable target for arrest. I do not believe that mass arrests would have been possible in the months immediately following the genocide. But targeted action against key individuals was possible. Instead the UN focused almost entirely on the humanitarian crisis caused by the outflow of refugees because it was something relatively easy, something the world was used to: masses of people needing food and shelter. In responding to the refugee crisis the bureaucrats in New York were able to salve the consciences of member nations. Having failed pitifully to act during the genocide, food drops, refugee camps and pious words were used to give the impression that something was being done about Rwanda. In the meantime Gacumbitsi and thousands like him were allowed to get away with murder. It was as if the genocide was being swept to one side, something regrettable that happened in the past, an African 'thing' that would be sorted out in an African way later on. All that mattered now was the crisis of the displaced, something that could be treated with traditional methods in full view of the world's television cameras. It was hard not to agree with the RPF when they accused the world of giving comfort to butchers.

That night we leave Tanzania, making the border just before it shuts down for the night. The policeman on duty sits at his desk with his head in his hands. The room is hot and stuffy because the overhead fan is broken. Outside the main door there are several rusting vehicles. They have been confiscated by the customs and are in the process of being cannibalized for spare parts. The policeman looks up and takes my passport. His eyes are bloodshot and there is a film of sweat on his forehead. He shakes his head. 'Malaria,' he says, placing my passport on the table. The man is in a bad way. I go outside and fetch some tablets and a bottle of water. He takes them gratefully and then slumps forward on his desk, pushing the passport into my hand. 'You can go, just please go,' he says. We are going back into Rwanda and night is coming on. I do not want to go back. I think the others feel the same because everybody is quiet. As we cross the bridge at Rusomo Falls, I look to the left, where the Tanzanian army has set up a small post. They are supposed to be checking for weapons on people crossing to and from Rwanda. But I see a group of soldiers stealing clothes and food from two refugees. The two must be on their way back into Rwanda and are probably Tutsis. There is something perverse about the sight of these armed soldiers rummaging through the belongings of the refugees.

Halfway across the bridge we stop to take some shots of the river, sending the drivers ahead to the Rwandan border. As Glenn and Tony film, the Tanzanians approach. Strictly speaking we are on the Rwandan side of the bridge, but they keep coming towards us, an officer at the front of a group of three soldiers. All carry automatic rifles. 'What are you doing, taking film of our positions?' the officer demands. He says he is a lieutenant and demands to see the film. Glenn says no. 'All I've filmed is the river, man, nothing else.' But we know that in one of the wide shots he might have caught a glimpse of the military. Perhaps they think we filmed them robbing the refugees. A small sergeant with a scar on the left side of his face walks up to the camera and begins to berate Glenn. The sergeant is drunk; I can smell the beer on his breath from several yards away. He does not speak English, but I think he is warning Glenn and Tony to get away from the camera. David is trying to persuade the lieutenant that we have no interest in filming the Tanzanian army. But the man wants to arrest us and take our tapes. These are the tapes of Gacumbitsi. 'You could be spies for the KGB or the CIA. Quite easily you could be,' he says. The lieutenant speaks good English but his mood swings dangerously. One moment I think we are reaching him, the next he is raving about foreign spies. 'You have a choice. You can go on your way and give us the tapes or you can all come with us,' he snaps. In the meantime the sergeant is giving Glenn and Tony a hard time. I look at Glenn and notice that he is worried. This situation is out of control. It will be dark soon and I do not want to be here with a neurotic lieutenant and his drunken sergeant. The sergeant becomes more belligerent. He wants to take us away and question

us. If this happens we are in serious trouble. I have seen enough
of drunken soldiers with guns to know that they are the most
dangerous people in the world. I ask the officer to step to one side.
'Please believe me we have no intention of harming Tanzania
and we are certainly not spies. However, if anything were to
happen to us, there would be terrible repercussions between the
government of Britain and your government.' I am trying pressure
now because soft words have got me nowhere and we are running
out of time. Then David steps in and protests our innocence
again. It is like working in shifts, pleading for our release. The
lieutenant stops and goes over to his drunken subordinate. They
huddle together for a few minutes. As this is going on, I notice a
familiar figure striding towards us across the bridge. 'Thank
God,' says Tony. It is Lieutenant Frank Ndore of the RPF,
keeping an appointment he had made with us several days before,
punctual almost to the minute. David fills him in on what has
been happening and he walks back to the Rwandan side of the
bridge to fetch one of his comrades. This younger man knows the
Tanzanians. He wheels and deals with them every day on behalf
of returning Tutsi refugees. The soldier begins a long discussion
with the Tanzanians. Although they are speaking Swahili, I
can tell that he is cajoling them. There is some laughter. Then
the discussions become serious again. The lieutenant turns around
and says he is leaving us in the care of the sergeant. There is
nothing more he can do. 'Oh, fuck, what now,' says Glenn. I
turn immediately to Frank. 'Jesus, Frank, don't leave us here
with this bastard. He is in the mood to do us serious harm.' I am
pleading. 'There is no way I am going to leave you guys here,

but just give our man a chance. That lieutenant has left for a reason. He doesn't want to be part of what's going to happen next. He knows the sergeant wants a bribe and that's why he has gone away. Our man is just negotiating the terms.' After a half an hour or so of haggling we part with several hundred US dollars. Frank advised us to hold out longer and try and beat the sergeant down, but I wasn't prepared to take the chance. We all wanted away from the border as fast as possible. The money is passed to the Tanzanians, who slouch back over the bridge, the sergeant turning to smirk at us. Frank apologizes and says he'll report the matter to the RPF's foreign affairs section. 'Those cunts. They rip off our people every day of the week and now they steal from you. They give Africa a bad name,' he fumes.

CHAPTER SIX

Siege

First one peacock. It appears from behind one of the twin colonnades that support the entrance to the palace of the president. It screams and is answered by a second bird that pick-picks its way across the broken glass of the courtyard. The birds move together towards the hedgerow, now overgrown, where the president's wife, Agathe, once used to delight foreign visitors with her knowledge of plants and flowers. She would not be pleased to see what is happening to her garden: the wild grasses are strangling her pretty flowers, there are strange new weeds shooting up in the rockeries, and there are thin, tough Tutsi boys with automatic rifles stalking the grounds while her peacocks cry out to the empty, humid air. Soon a hungry soldier will take it into his head to kill these screeching ornaments and prepare them for the pot. The RPF military commander, Paul Kagame, has given strict instructions that nothing be looted. Those who disobey risk severe punishment. Yet even with such orders I am amazed that the birds have lasted this long. Most other guerrilla armies would have devoured them a long time ago. In the middle of the courtyard, almost directly in front of the main door of the palace, lies an empty Dom Perignon bottle. On closer examination I see that there is a small well of liquid in which float several dead wasps. The soldier who is guiding us can be no more than fifteen. Frank has decided to wait outside in the car. He has already seen the presidential palace several times. 'Going in there just makes me feel fucking angry,' he says. There is broken glass everywhere but the rooms on the ground floor have been left remarkably unscathed by the fighting that took place around the compound. The palace is right next to the airport and the big military base of Kanombe. Habyarimana knew a thing or two about self-preservation. He built his home right next to a secure airstrip, and then stuffed thousands of his most loyal troops into a base alongside. Try to imagine his shock when early on the night of 6 April, as his jet was approaching the airport, the lights of his home twinkling below, two huge explosions smashed into the aircraft and sent it crashing into the garden of the palace. A French magazine with links to the Habyarimana family has published photographs of the crash victims: the president lies under a blanket, though his bloodied head is uncovered; an army commander travelling with him lies on the gravel, his face detached from his head and lying on the ground like a mask.

The wreckage of the plane is half inside, half outside the palace gardens. There is a long section of the wing, parts of the engine and fuselage, lumps and scraps of metal glinting in the dying afternoon sun. There are a number of craters. The biggest is like a First World War shell-hole. There is nothing left of the dead, save perhaps a fragment of bone embedded deep in the earth *and hidden from our eyes. The plane missed the president's house by only a short distance. His killers must have hidden in the banana groves that run between the palace and the army base at Kanombe. They would have seen the plane come in low over the hills, its navigation lights flashing as it approached the airport where the president's guard detail awaited. And then, with minutes to go before landing, they fired. There were perhaps two rockets that slammed into the Falcon jet and signalled the beginning of the Rwandan apocalypse. The most important part of the plane, the cockpit black box, has disappeared. Months later a French spook with links to the Habyarimana family will surface with such a box, claiming that it proves the RPF were behind the attack. But he produces no proof and nobody believes him and after a while he vanishes from public view. The rebels make no attempt to interfere with our filming and examination of the wreckage. Nor have they made any attempt to stop numerous other journalists who have passed through here. As we walk from the garden into the house, there is a sound like thunder coming from the direction of the city. 'Artillery and mortars,' says Glenn, 'it's all right man . . . it's going the right way, away from us.' I am thankful for the military training that the South African Defence Force has bestowed on Glenn. I have always had difficulty telling the difference between incoming and outgoing until the last moment when the shells actually start falling near by. I think that is a product of pure fear. Once the bangs start I don't give a damn where they are coming from, I just want to get down and safe as quickly as possible.*

The rumbling from the city fades as we walk into the

presidential reception room. David takes the crew upstairs while I wander in the empty rooms. There are deep pile carpets, mock regency chairs, endless gold leaf, enough china and crystal to cater for armies . . . yet the army that now occupies the palace has not touched one iota of this treasure trove. There has been a single act of deliberate vandalism: the portrait of Habyarimana and his wife has been defaced. Somebody has taken a bayonet and driven it into the dead president's eyes. In the photograph he is smiling, but there are two white spaces where the eyes once shone.

The palace fish tanks have been neglected by the rebels. In the weeks of slaughter the water has turned green and the tropical fish have sunk to the bottom, where they lie rotting among the flourishing algae and scores of water lice. From the kitchen there is a smell of curry powder and herbs, the scent of the latter grassy and sharp. Somebody has opened the herb jar and left it to lie in the sun. The kitchen table is a scrapyard of dirty dishes, empty tins, mouldy lumps of food. Here I suspect the rebels have helped themselves to whatever was left in Mrs Habyarimana's cupboards, for I can find nothing save some bottles of sauce, a packet of flour and the sun-withered herbs. Upstairs there is more broken glass where a grand chandelier has come crashing down on to the landing. I can hear David, Glenn and Tony on the third floor. They are climbing towards Habyarimana's rooftop chapel, where the big man is said to have prayed every day. I wander into the president's daughter's bedroom, where there are piles of clothes scattered across the floor. Her underwear has been rooted out of drawers and lies on the large white bed along with dresses and shoes, many, many pairs of shoes.

The young rebel who has been assigned to guide us reappears. I ask him what he thinks of the palace but he just shrugs. Then I realize that he speaks no English. From his age and lack of English I imagine he must be a recent recruit, one of the young boys who, like Valence, has seen his family wiped out and decided to fight back. He motions towards a room at the other side of the hall, smiling. I follow him through two large bedrooms, those of the president and his wife, into a small study of dark wood and soft carpeting. On the floor there are scores of shotgun cartridges and other bigger bullets. When Glenn appears from upstairs a few minutes later I ask him what the big bullets are for. 'Elephant bullets – they'd put a hole the size of a barn door into you,' he says. Then David explains that Habyarimana was a big-game hunter; blasting animals to kingdom come was one of his great delights. Whole national parks would be closed off while the president and his entourage went shooting. While Habyarimana enjoyed the kill, his brother-in-law Protais Zigi-ranyirazo was up to his neck in the trade in endangered species. Protais was a founder member of the Zero Network and an original shareholder of Radio Mille Collines. A book David has brought with him on our journey, Murder in the Mist, alleges that Protais was involved in the murder of American naturalist Diane Fossey because of her attempts to save the gorillas of the Rwandan rain forest. To date he has not even issued a rebuttal, much less attempted to sue the author. Protais is currently enjoying the sanctuary provided by the government of France, along with his sister Agathe and several other family members. It is not likely that they will see the palace ever again, but they have the security of foreign bank accounts and the sympathy of the Quai d'Orsay (French Foreign Ministry) to console them in exile. I can see what sickens Frank. This place reeks of greed and death; this was the nucleus of Hutu extremism until the people around the president decided that Habyarimana had become a threat to their power. The palace should be left to decay, season after season, with the bush growing thick and wild, until it vanishes under a canopy of green. The grounds outside the palace are littered with ammunition. Belts of heavy machine-gun bullets, crates of shells and grenades and scores of Rwandan army helmets. Glenn checks the ammunition and the grenades and recognizes them from his South African army days. Most of the stuff here is either South African or French. The matériel from down south is the product of Armscor – the huge state arms corporation established to circumvent the UN ban on weapons sales to South Africa during the apartheid era. We have all known for several months that Pretoria's guns and bullets were being shipped north to the Rwandan army. But seeing it here, just weeks after watching Mandela being sworn in as president of a non-racial nation, makes those of us who live in South Africa feel uneasy, even ashamed.

Outside the gates Frank and Valence are waiting to escort us back to the cars. Valence, who has been very quiet since we left Nyarubuye, is smiling again. Frank says he thinks Valence has found a girl in Kigali and we all laugh, walking towards the cars and the muffled sound of explosions in the valley below.

★

Kigali in the early days of June was a city bathed in the blood of past and current massacres. Since the killing had begun on 6 April Rwanda's capital had been the setting for butchery on a massive scale. Hundreds of thousands of Tutsis and many Hutus who opposed the government had either been murdered in their homes or stopped at road-blocks and hacked to death. Kigali had been the epicentre of the genocide. Although the suburbs we drove through were largely empty of people, with the rubble of war still strewn across the roads, it was possible in the golden evening light to think of Kigali as having once been a pleasant city. From where we stood on the heights held by the RPF, Kigali seemed to be surrounded by mountains and hills. There were many flowers, bougainvillaea and hibiscus and countless others whose names were unknown to me, blossoming in the hedges. The red-tiled roofs of some of the bungalows gave the city a Mediterranean aspect. There was no sign of the vast slum dwellings of Kinshasa or the concrete blockhouses of Nairobi or the skyscrapers of Johannesburg. The avenues off the main road were dirt tracks but there were rows of trees that gave them a secluded, peaceful ambience. This delusion lasted only as long as you stayed in the Land Rover and did not wander through the empty houses. Because out there in the sun-shine, mingling with the scent of the new flowers, was the old scent of death. David, Glenn and Tony had followed the smell on our first day in Kigali. They had gone into the ruins of a café that had been burned out in the looting that followed Habyarimana's assassination. Lying on the ground were three people, hands tied behind their backs, massive wounds to their heads. From the state of decomposition it looked as if they had been lying there since the early days of the genocide. The rebels had sent body squads into the ruins in an attempt to prevent the spread of disease. But with so many dead in houses and streets across the city and a full-scale siege under way, they were never going to be able to gather in all the corpses. I had thought that after Nyarubuye the smell of death would have lost some of its fearful potency for me. But I still churned inside every time we passed a place of execution.

On the day we arrived in Kigali one half of the city was still in government hands. We could see the smoke from mortar rounds landing in the government sector in the valley below. Occasionally the ground would thunder near our position, signalling the arrival of a government shell. Somewhere in the jumble of houses, offices and churches on the government side were thousands of Tutsis waiting for death at the hands of the army and the Interahamwe. These were people who had survived the first wave of killings but who now faced certain extermination. In the tightly controlled government area there were no secure hiding places. The RPF was attempting to infiltrate snatch squads into the government-held sector of the city to rescue the Tutsis. But Frank warned us that any attempt to travel into the government area on our own would be suicidal. 'These fuckers don't care what you are. They just want to kill. And if you don't have UN protection they will cut your throats,' he said. Technically speaking the job of securing the release of refugees fell to the UN. It did manage to arrange a number of evacuations. But by and large the few hundred soldiers of the UN based in Kigali were impotent in the face of the slaughter. The force had been cut, under pressure from Belgium and the Americans, from 2,500 soldiers to 250, and they were confined to Kigali once the killing started. By the time I arrived in Kigali – early June – the local force commanders were still waiting for the armoured vehicles they needed to mount patrols in the city. The Americans were insisting on higher rental terms for the vehicles than the UN would pay. Most of the RPF soldiers I met had contempt for the UN. Every day during the week I spent in Kigali, the RPF's commanders would arrive at the UN buildings and sit down opposite senior officers of the Rwandan army, or Forces Armées Rwandaises (FAR). The UN would tell the journalists that a meeting had taken place but would not even bother to claim that it had been 'frank and useful' – the stock diplomatic phrase for meetings that have gone nowhere. As they sat eyeballing the genocidal warriors of the FAR, the guerrillas had one objective in mind: total defeat of the government. The RPF had learned from the past. Nobody had come to rescue the Tutsis when they were slaughtered in 1959, or again in the purges of the seventies. Nobody was going to come this time even if there was ample evidence that the Hutu extremists were planning to wipe the Tutsis off the face of the earth. The Americans were dithering over whether to use the word 'genocide' and haggling over the terms for the hire of armoured cars to the UN force; the Belgians had pulled their troops out after ten soldiers had been disarmed and tortured to death; the French were supplying the government side; Britain said little and did nothing; and the countries of Africa shouted loud but were also doing little. In such circumstances the RPF concluded that nothing short of total victory would be enough to save Rwanda's remaining Tutsis and wrest the country from the hands of the extremists.

Don't get me wrong. There were many brave soldiers wearing the blue helmet of the UN in Kigali. But they were too few in number, too poorly armed and had a mandate that turned them into little more than spectators to the slaughter. One of the first people I met at the UN headquarters was a burly Ghanaian officer named Emmanuel Quist. Quist was the deputy chief of operations and a frank, open-minded man. 'This here is evil. What we are seeing is pure evil,' he told me on the day we met. Quist described the first day of the killing. He was in a building near the airport with several of his men. On the morning after the crash he was shaving near a balcony overlooking the roadway. Outside there was a roadblock. After a while a man came up to the roadblock and his papers were examined by a gang of young toughs with machetes. Without saying a word they pulled him to one side and he was struck with a machete and knocked to the ground. Some of Quist's soldiers started shouting. All they could do was shout. Their mandate did not allow them to intervene militarily. So they shouted and screamed. They were very emotional. Some of them were crying. The Ghanaian troops could not believe what they were seeing. The killers waited for a few minutes and then pulled the man down a lane to finish him off. A short while later another man was seized and the same thing happened. After that Quist stopped watching. Although he could not say it on the record, Quist wanted me to know that he was sick to his stomach of the whole thing. The officers under his command were doing their best but they had no protection and nobody in New York was going to thank them for getting killed. The gruesome killing of the ten Belgians had spooked everyone. There were bad stories doing the rounds about what they had suffered, castration and all kinds of torture. Their vehicle was awash with blood when it was recovered soon after the killings. And then came the killing of a well-respected and popular Senegalese officer, taken out by a rebel shell near the front line. No man had worked harder or more patiently on behalf of refugees trapped behind both armies. But the shell that landed near his car made no distinction between the good and the bad. There were a lot of evil men near by who might have taken the round but it wiped out one of the most decent people in the city. After that nobody was in the mood to take chances. Lt Colonel Quist was looking forward to going home.

The UN building became a workstation for the journalists covering the siege. There was a BBC satellite phone and there were NATO rations – a vital food source in a city that had been looted as thoroughly as Kigali. Occasionally there was some information: confirmation of a fresh massacre or news of rebel advances elsewhere in the country. Mostly, however, there was nothing to say. The man charged with saying it was a tough and dour French Canadian, Major Guy Plante. Plante was not the most sociable of men but he had a reputation for fair play among the correspondents who were sitting out the full duration of the siege and who dealt with him on a day-to-day basis.

One morning at the height of the siege Plante came storming into the press room and offered a facility. 'Anybody wants to go to the Red Cross Hospital, now is your chance. We're leaving in five minutes,' he barked, before marching off to the main operations room. We scrambled into flak jackets and piled into the two white UN vehicles outside. 'Keep the camera down. Down between your knees. We don't know how these Interahamwe at the roadblock will react if they see that thing,' he told Glenn. Glenn took one look at the expression on Plante's face and immediately buried the camera under his legs. My BBC colleague Mark Doyle had made this journey a few times, but he was as nervous as the rest of us. It occurred to me that his fear was the result of those previous journeys. Doyle had been in Kigali long enough to understand just how dangerous a place it could be. After the last rebel roadblock we headed out on to an open stretch of road in full view of gunners from both sides. It was somewhere along here that the Senegalese officer, a friend of Mark Doyle's, was killed the previous week. Plante drove very fast and I could tell that the silence and emptiness of the road unnerved him as much as it did the rest of us. After seven or eight minutes we arrived at the first roadblock on the government side. These were soldiers, young toughs wearing the beret insignia of the presidential guard and gathered around a jeep. They waved us through quickly and we turned and drove up a steep road. There were people walking towards us carrying bags and blankets on their heads: refugees heading away from the fighting towards what was left of government-held Rwanda in the south-west. Plante turned a sharp left and we came to an immediate stop. The men at the roadblock wore ragged clothes and carried machetes. I saw bottles of half-drunk beer on the ground. 'Fucking charming customers,' whispered Tony. Plante rolled the window down and spoke to them in French. I wondered how many Tutsis had died at this roadblock, how many more were desperately hiding out in this area.

I can only remember the face of one man. He had wild matted hair, his eyes were red, and he reeked of beer and old sweat. He scowled at Plante and then slowly moved his barricade of beer crates. Tony's voice hissed in my ear again: 'Can you just imagine what it's like to be a Tutsi coming up against a roadblock with the likes of that bastard on it?' I couldn't imagine what it would be like. The stomach-churning fear and then, as your identity card was seized, the certainty of death. In the preceding weeks tens of thousands of Tutsis had spent their last moments of life at such roadblocks.

The hospital was surrounded by militiamen and soldiers. They milled about in the road, eyeing us warily as we walked to the main gate. Just outside the gate several soldiers lay on stretchers. They had been wounded in the past hour. An army medic had covered them with blankets while they waited for admission to the hospital. Most of them seemed to have suffered shrapnel wounds, but they seemed more scared than seriously injured. The RPF had been pounding their base all morning, rockets crashing down from the heights above the city. As we waited for the gate to open, there was a loud explosion. Everybody ducked. A mortar round had landed very close by. I heard David's voice above the shouting voices. 'Did we get that, Glenn?' he asked. 'I think so. Hard to tell when you're running for your life,' came the tart reply. The hospital had been hit several times already. Just two days before we arrived seven people were killed when a shell landed in one of the recovery wards.

I had visited one of the rebel mortar positions a couple of days previously and met an articulate young officer who rejoiced in the name of Colonel K.K. Caesar. It was his job to direct and co-ordinate fire on the government positions. He stood on the hill above the city, calling out co-ordinates to two teams of mortar men. I looked through his binoculars and saw the distant, tiny figures of government soldiers running for cover along a lane in the heart of the city. When I asked him if he was worried that there might be civilian casualties, he told me there were no civilians left in the areas controlled by the Rwandan army. But wasn't the bombardment causing massive destruction, I wondered. His reply was practised and calm: 'In all wars things have to be destroyed. In order to rid this country of the genocidal forces there are things that have to be destroyed. This is a war against evil.' Standing outside the Red Cross Hospital, I wondered if he were the one directing the bombardment down on top of us.

There was an argument at the gate. An army officer was demanding to be allowed into the hospital. The orderly was refusing to let him in. The soldier paced back and forth in front of the small steel gate. He was growing impatient and jabbed his index finger in the direction of the orderly every few seconds. The military regularly attempted to enter the hospital to abduct patients, people who might have survived the initial apocalypse and whose presence inside the hospital had been betrayed by a wounded soldier or militiaman. A nurse appeared and took the officer to one side. I have no idea what she said but the man nodded his head and went away. After that the lock was opened and we were ushered into the hospital compound. I had never seen such overcrowding. The wounded and dying lay everywhere. A constant procession of stretchers moved up and down the stairs between the two levels of the hospital. Those on the ground floor near the gate and the operating theatre were mostly soldiers. Some were suffering from terrible wounds. Blood seeped through bandages. One man whose leg had been blown off lay staring at the sky, his face fixed in a half smile. I supposed that he must have been given morphine and was at that moment drifting above the pain and suffering. It was possible to look into the operating theatre through a window near the admissions area. Inside three white doctors were busy amputating a leg that had been ravaged by shrapnel. The men looked exhausted, the sweat pouring down their faces as they cut their way through tissue and bone. A woman was carried through with deep red lines down her thighs. Shrapnel again, this time a grenade that had sent shards of metal flying up into her groin.

There was a sound of crying from the upper level. We climbed the stairs and saw a woman rolling on the ground. A Swiss doctor and a black nurse were trying to calm her. I could not see a wound because the woman was wrapped in a blanket. 'Mon dieu, oh, mon dieu,' she called out. One of the workers said the woman was suffering from shell-shock. The constant explosions had pushed her over the edge. A white woman doctor spent several minutes trying to comfort her, but she moaned and cried continually and in the end was left alone. There was nothing to be done and there were others with more urgent problems. Next to where she lay was a tent filled with children. Although the Red Cross did its best to protect the ethnic identities of its patients, I could tell these were mostly Tutsi infants. They had been wounded with knives and clubs. There was a small boy whose arm had been cut off. Flies crawled around the bandage. The child had been given a present of a jigsaw of Africa, which sat on his lap. The countries were jumbled around on the blanket and with his one good arm he picked out one after another, and attempted to complete the jigsaw.

There were several other tents and a long ward packed with wounded people. The Red Cross workers were dealing with hundreds of casualties every day but they were managing to preserve hygiene. In such confined conditions, with a war raging all around, an epidemic of typhoid or cholera would have wiped out everybody in days. The doctors were operating around the clock, living in fear of shell-fire and the militias. Although they would have eschewed any such suggestion, I found it hard not to regard them as heroes. Dr Jean Marie Chapatte, a young Swiss doctor, shook his head sadly when I asked him if he understood what was going on. 'To understand? No, that is not possible at the moment. Now I have just to do my work, get on with things. But to understand is not possible. Maybe later, but not now.' The doctor wanted to know why people kept fighting around the hospital when they knew it was occupied by the Red Cross. 'Everybody knows we are neutral,' he said. But I suspect he knew as well as I did that in Rwanda's unfolding horror story, nobody much cared about the sanctity of a hospital building. There was a shout from downstairs. 'Come on now, now, we leave now, now.' It was the voice of Major Plante urging us on. 'Do you want to be left here?' he called out. David hurried off to placate the Canadian while I went back to the children's tent with Glenn and Tony. In a few moments David was back. 'Something is up. We have to get out of here now.' He looked deadly serious. David was not the kind of man given to exaggeration or panic. When he appeared with a strained look like that on his face, we knew it was time to move quickly. 'What the fuck is going on?' Glenn gasped, as we headed down the stairs towards the gate. The answer appeared in the form of two haggard-looking white men, who were standing huddled behind the other journalists and the great bulky figure of Major Plante. The men seemed frightened. One of them wore his arm in a sling. David explained what was happening: 'These two missionary brothers have just escaped from the militia. Their only way out is to go with us, pretend that they are journalists. The UN thinks the army or the Interahamwe will kill them if they try to make it alone. We are their cover.' I wanted to ask what would happen if the Interahamwe stopped us and searched the vehicles. What would they do to us if they found us sheltering the brothers? And then I stopped myself asking

132

such questions. Not because they made me more afraid, but because they made me feel ashamed. These men were vulnerable and alone and needed help. God alone knew what they had been through in the past few weeks. I told myself to have confidence in Plante and then walked over and shook hands with the brothers. Plante told us to huddle together around them and then follow him to the vehicles. There were curious stares as we moved through the gate and down to the cars. We chatted self-consciously until we were inside and the engine was switched on. The brothers were travelling in the second vehicle. Plante reckoned that once the first was waved through, the second would be allowed to follow on without hassle. He was correct. For fifteen sweaty, nerve-racking minutes we negotiated our way back across the city, but there were no problems. I felt like breaking into song when the first rebel checkpoints appeared.

The two brothers were members of the African Missionaries, a French order that had been working in Rwanda for many years. Brother Henri Blanchard was a diminutive figure who wore steel-rimmed glasses perched on his gaunt, pale face. He was balding, with wisps of hair plastered back across his head. The other priest was German. Brother Otto Meyer was taller than his colleague with a full red beard and bright blue eyes. He was the younger of the two and seemed less haunted in appearance than Brother Henri. Brother Otto had been wounded by shrapnel the previous week and had worn his arm in a sling since then. They were going to be evacuated out of Rwanda via Kampala in the next forty-eight hours but neither wanted to go. After eating and washing they gave a press conference at the UN headquarters and described the massacres that had erupted in the aftermath of the president's death. Although tired they answered questions with great patience. What they described was much the same story as had been told by the few refugees who had escaped from the government sector of the city in the last few days. The massacres were continuing. People, especially young men, were being abducted every day. I sensed that from behind the very calm recitation of facts there was another story. The brothers had left something behind in the government sector. That evening I went back to see them.

The militia have been killing all week. Brother Otto looks out the window of his room at St Paul's Church and sees that the pile of bodies has been getting bigger and bigger. The other day prisoners in pink uniform came and picked up a huge load of corpses. But they will have to come again. Somebody said they come every three days. He hopes so. It is too much to believe, this mound of corpses. The smell from the bodies is bad. It covers everything these days. Brother Otto has seen things that no training could have prepared him for. 'The brutality, the brutality of these young thugs. They think they can solve their problems by killing the other ethnic group.' But it's not just the youngsters. The army are much worse. The other day he saw soldiers throwing stones at the children to rouse them into killing. Some of them did not want to kill but the army forced them to take part. Everybody must have blood on their hands. Then no one person can be blamed. The German brother has worked here for years. He thought he knew these people. What did he know? 'There is a madness at work. They kill and then steal everything. They want to be like the rich, like the government people. Kill the head of the household and take what he owns.'

The killing goes on and on. Otto has been wounded now and he cannot stay at St Paul's. There is shrapnel in his arm. But if he leaves what will happen to the Tutsi orphans who are hiding in the house? His friend Brother Henri has been holding the militia off for days. Henri is small but a tough man. He faces up to them and says, 'Kill me but leave the children alone.' So far they have not taken him up on the offer. But if they wanted to, the Interahamwe could come in and kill all of them. If they leave, the orphans will die; if they do not, Otto may not survive. The children know this and they start to become very frightened. The brothers decide that they must leave. Otto's wound is getting worse and the fighting is intensifying. Inside, Otto is churning up. He wonders how he ended up in this situation. He had come to Africa because he believed in the power of God's word. But where was the good here? What a world where children are hiding because death is edging closer and closer to them. Henri talks to the children and prays with them. They know what is coming and so they ask a favour. 'Brother, please lock us in the room. If you lock us in here, they will not find us. Please lock us in.' It is as if the children understand that there is no choice. All choices have been removed.

And so looking at their faces for the last time, Henri closes the door and locks them in. There is no food to give them. The supplies have run out. Henri and Otto leave. They leave the children.

Now, as he is telling me the story, Henri starts to weep. He places his hand underneath his glasses and rubs his eyes, but he cannot stop crying. Henri is looking into the wide frightened eyes of the orphans. He is hearing their voices as he walks down the corridor away from the room. Beside him Otto sits with a look in his eyes that begs my understanding. 'We were overwhelmed, you see. We were overwhelmed by this great evil, by these acts of wickedness,' he says. Henri then speaks: 'Somebody said to me that when they got out of Rwanda they would be insane. As for me . . . I am left with lifelong questions. What did I do that I should not have done? What did I not do that I should have done?' I take Brother Henri's hand and try to comfort him. These brothers feel a terrible guilt, but they are good men. Overwhelmed. Yes, that is the word for what has happened to them. Overwhelmed. On 14 June, a week after the rescue of the brothers, the militia murdered fifty men and boys who had been seized from the church.

That night we stayed in a comfortable bungalow close to Colonel Caesar's mortar position. Every few minutes we could hear the sound of rounds being dispatched into the city. Moses and Edward were nervous. The older driver knew from his years in the Ugandan army that when one group of soldiers shelled another, the favour was frequently returned. He had shared this information with Edward, who had become sullen and edgy. With each loud bang he would twitch and mutter to himself. The house must have been the home of a wealthy businessman or a highly placed government employee. There were four bedrooms, a large sitting-room, a well-equipped kitchen and a generous garden full of bougainvillaea and herbs. There was also a black Labrador who had been abandoned when the owners fled. The animal was painfully thin but frolicked and played with anybody who paid it attention. Standing on the porch, I could see occasional puffs of white smoke down in the valley where the RPF shells were landing. So far the government side had failed to pinpoint Colonel Caesar's position. Glenn had noticed the nervousness of the drivers and produced a roll of masking tape. He went to the room we had been allocated at the back of the house and began to tape the windows. 'The house might come down on top of us, guys, but you won't cut your hands,' he said, grinning as he sealed the glass. It was a sensible precaution. A direct hit you could do nothing about. But what Glenn was trying to save us from was the spray of glass that would result from a round that landed near by. Once again I had cause to thank his South African military training. As it grew dark the RPF began firing Katyusha rockets. These Russian-made weapons scream when they are launched, descending on the enemy in a fury of explosive power. The shrieking sound in the gathering dark unnerved everybody. Tony went to the room and produced a bottle of whisky. Somebody else found some beers and a bottle of red wine. I went into the kitchen and raided the presses of the recently departed owners. Herbs, stock cubes, rice and pasta. This was one way of touching base with a kind of normality, a means of keeping fear at bay. Frank appeared at the doorway, smiling. 'You gonna cook for us again tonight. You're too good, my man. You really are too good.'

He was chiding me gently. David and I had pushed Frank hard, taking him back to places he would rather forget and dragging him into our dispute with the Tanzanians. Through it all he had been patient and understanding. There was no attempt to stop us doing our job or to brainwash us. Frank was too intelligent a man to act simply as a propagandist for the RPF. He knew that the scenes we had witnessed spoke volumes more than any party political lecture. Instead he gave advice when asked and he kept us safe. I spoke to him about music and books and women and discovered a man who should have been lecturing in a university, not fighting a war. That night after eating we sat out on the balcony with a bottle of whisky between us and an endless supply of cigarettes. The shelling was less intense, although I could still see huge flashes far away to the south. I asked Frank if they had brought in big guns to shell Gitarama, where the Rwandan interim government had fled in the past few days. 'No, that is only thunder. That is so far away it could be over Lake Tanganyika.' And then without prompting Frank began to speak about the madness that had descended on the country of his ancestors.

'This is about power, Fergal. It is about one bunch of people who don't want to share power and those of us who believe that we shouldn't be excluded from the running of this country. We are Rwandans. They can't keep up this fucking mythology that we are Ugandans, foreigners. I have a right to be here. The RPF has a right to be here. Now there is only one way to finish this. The killers must be defeated, completely and totally. If you compromise with people like this you are finished. They will be at your throat in a few weeks, maybe even a few days' time.'

'You say it's about power, Frank,' I said, 'but that doesn't explain to me why so many ordinary Hutus just got up and killed their neighbours. Not all of them were forced to do it. I mean, there are hundreds of thousands dead. You can't say there isn't an ethnic dimension. A lot of people hated the Tutsis and really wanted to kill. Didn't they?'

Frank took a draught from his cup of whisky before answering. 'Look, sure there were feelings of resentment. It's what I would call an inferiority complex, which a lot of Hutu peasants still have. Like something inside which says, "The Tutsis are better than us and even worse they think they are better than us." And you get poor people like that with those kind of feelings and then somebody comes along and starts to whip them up and say, "If only the Tutsis were sorted out" or "All this trouble and poverty is all the fault of the RPF and that is a Tutsi organization", well, then you have a really dangerous situation.'

'But aren't you really a Tutsi organization?' I responded.

'No. I am sick of people calling us Tutsis. I told you before I don't give a fuck what a man is. I care about politics, not ethnicity. All this obsession with size and appearance, it just hides the real truth of what is happening here. There are Hutus in the RPF, not many I admit, but they are there.'

I agreed that everybody I had met in the RPF had gone out of his or her way to stress the importance of politics over ethnicity. But surely the problem now was that the RPF would be ruling an empty country. Hutus didn't trust them.

'It is true that the minds of ordinary Hutus are being poisoned against us. They are being told that we will kill them like they killed our people. It's not going to happen that way. We want to get the big killers and deal with them. But we can't go around putting every single peasant in jail and we don't want to do that. We have Hutu politicians who survived the massacres and they will be part of the new government of national unity. Just give us a chance. Tell the world to give us a chance and stop recognizing that bunch of bastards who carried out the genocide.'

At the time of our conversation the Rwandan seat at the UN was held by the government side. This at a time when

Boutros Boutros Ghali was publicly speaking of his shame at the world's failure to intervene in Rwanda. Like most RPF officers Frank had little faith in the UN as an organization, yet he had never sought to interfere in our frequent contacts with UN staff in Kigali. Given the failure of the UN in New York to act against the slaughter of the Tutsis, Frank's open-mindedness was admirable.

After finishing the bottle of whisky we decided it was time to sleep. Tomorrow we would be saying goodbye. Frank was heading off for a meeting with the RPF leadership, and we were preparing to leave for Burundi on a journey that would ultimately take us into the small area of Rwanda that remained in government hands. I wanted to give him a gift but I could think of nothing. There were some cigarettes and some whisky, but they did not seem adequate mementoes of our journey. And then I remembered my book of Yeats poems. I found them at the bottom of my rucksack and presented them to Frank. I could not think of what to say at that last moment and so I mumbled 'good luck' and pushed the book into his hands.

'Take it easy,' he said. 'Maybe we can meet in Ireland sometime and get drunk and you can introduce me to an Irish girl.'

'And one for Valence too,' I said.

'Yes, one for Valence. We will laugh then, my friend,' he replied.

And we shook hands and hugged and said goodnight.

★

Two last memories of Kigali. The Amahoro Stadium close to where we are staying: there are thousands of refugees crammed in here, protected by the UN. This is a mixed group of Hutus and Tutsis. Before the rebels came it was nearly all Tutsis and the Interahamwe would come night after night and take people away. Now the refugees have the shelling to worry about. Several rounds have fallen inside and killed people. Amahoro means 'independence' and in the old days Habyarimana and his clique would parade before the adoring masses here. Now the stands are crowded with ragged and frightened people. A woman is reading a bible aloud and rocking back and forth. 'Excuse me,' I ask, 'are you Hutu or Tutsi?' She looks up at me and stares hard. There is a look of pure contempt in her eyes. She says nothing and I mumble an apology and leave.

And then the Mille Collines Hotel in the government sector: what remains of the city's educated and wealthier Tutsis are prisoners here. A Malaysian UN officer has taken us to the hotel in an armoured vehicle. People have been killed leaving and entering this building. There are worried faces staring out from the top windows. Some more people are standing around in the lobby. At the main door a presidential guardsman sits with a clipboard. He is taking the name of anyone who enters and leaves. There are guardsmen and Interahamwe loitering at the entrance and a handful of UN troops to keep them at bay. It is like watching a cat playing with a mouse. At any time the killers can go inside and pick a victim. They are simply toying with the soon to be dead. Goodbye, Kigali, may I never see you again.

CHAPTER SEVEN

Borderlands

Our new escort was a boy named Ernest. He also held the
rank of lieutenant but was at least five years younger than
Frank. An Italian television crew who had worked with
him threw their eyes up to heaven when we mentioned his
name. 'All he wants to do is sleep. It's no you can't do this,
no you can't do that,' one of them said. 'He is absolutely
useless.' Sure enough, when we did track Ernest down on
the morning we were to leave, he was fast asleep. Glenn and
Tony had spent most of the morning lying under one of
the Land Rovers with an Ethiopian mechanic. An ominous
rattling in the undercarriage had become obvious in the past
few days. The UN warned us against taking to the road
with a damaged vehicle. Getting stuck in the Rwandan
bush at night was not advisable. The Ethiopian thought we
would make it to Burundi without too much trouble.
Ernest seemed unconcerned. 'You will be all right,' he told
me, yawning as he retreated once more into the room
where he had been sleeping. Ernest had the appearance

of a novice monk. He had a thin face with large eyes, and silver-framed spectacles and a small goatee. When he spoke it was in a mumble. I was continually asking him to repeat himself. The other escort was a teenager who had joined the RPF only in the past month. He was bright-eyed and energetic with immense buck teeth that gave him an appearance of perpetual cheerfulness. But he spoke only Kinyarwanda and remained a mystery to us throughout the journey. Ernest claimed that he knew a safe and quick route into Burundi. He took David's map and drew what looked to me like an arbitrary line with his finger in the direction of the border. 'That is the way. It will not be a problem. We will make the other side by nightfall,' he promised. I looked along the supposed route of our journey and noticed that there didn't seem to be a single large town on the way. 'Do you have lots of troops in this area, Ernest?' I asked. 'Oh, of course. I am telling you there will be no problems,' he replied.

We took the road south from Kigali as far as the town of Kabuga. The streets were still littered with spent ammunition casings and the cast-off uniforms of government forces who had fled the rebel advance. Most of the buildings had been struck by machine-gun and shell fire. The population was dead or in exile. We stopped to record some of the images of war. I stepped into one building and saw the charred body of a government soldier. Somebody had tried to cover him with a piece of tarpaulin but had succeeded in blanketing only the upper half of the body.

His legs and toes, black and spindly, poked out from under the canvas. On the street outside I found a photograph album. A young man in army uniform posed with his girlfriend. She was wearing a bright yellow dress and carried a bouquet of flowers. Was this a wedding album? On other pages the soldier appeared with his family and friends. Several different groups of boys holding beers and smiling. Was he dead now? Was he the soldier rotting in the room I had just left? Had he been a killer of Tutsis? He certainly would have seen the killing. Everybody did.

The fighting here must have been particularly intense. Wandering through back alleys, I noticed the explosive punch marks of rocket-propelled grenades and shards of shrapnel sprayed along the pathways. Many of the buildings had been turned into powder. Huge sheets of corrugated iron had been twisted and gnarled by the explosions. The remains of a cow lay stinking, half in and half out of a doorway. Most of the people who lived in the town had been displaced in other parts of the country. Because Kabuga had a big rebel presence the refugees felt safer here than they would have in their homes in the more remote rural areas. By the time we left Kabuga it was well after lunch. Ernest believed it would take us three hours to reach the Burundi border. That would leave just enough time to get there before the Burundians shut down for the night. With any luck we would be in the Burundian capital Bujumbura in time to get a meal and then a long sleep between clean sheets. With thoughts of comfort and rest in mind we drove out of Kabuga along a side road, the route of Ernest's short-cut.

The road begins as tar. For about two miles beyond the town it loops and bends. But the going is smooth and I doze off. I am awakened by a rough grinding sound. We have moved on to a dirt track. 'Is this a main road into Burundi?' I ask Ernest. He does not reply. I think he is pretending not to hear me. I look at David, who seems unconcerned, and then I close my eyes again. In the half sleep I imagine that we are in a deep jungle with no sunlight. When David nudges me awake I can see that the bush on the roadside is growing thick and wild. It is leaning into the middle of the track and brushing against the windows of our cars. The afternoon heat is pure torture. There is not a breath of air and we are low on water. We are rationing ourselves. Two bottles for the journey among four of us, two RPF men and the two drivers. There are endless abandoned huts along the way. The countryside is empty again. We pass two fairly large villages that are deserted. There is the occasional whiff of bodies. Then Edward, who is driving the second car, begins to flash his lights. We grind to a halt in clouds of dust. He climbs under the car and spends the next fifteen minutes hammering and twisting a bolt under the steering wheel. Tony comes up to our vehicle. 'It looks like the UN guys didn't manage to fix it properly. All the shaking on the road is after making it go loose again. We're going to have to go very slowly, OK?' Moses nods his assent, but Ernest says nothing at all. His silence is starting to get on my nerves, but I am in no position to have an argument with him.

We are in the middle of nowhere. Only he knows which way to go and only he has a gun.

We set off again into a landscape of vast banana plantations. The vegetation here is the thickest, most verdant we have seen anywhere in Rwanda. Eventually we come to a small village. There are perhaps six mud cabins and a very bad smell. Beyond the village is a tiny bridge over a stream. The water looks clean and pure and we pause briefly to check on the car. Edward's repair job seems to be holding up. The stream is flowing out of a swamp that stretches ahead on the right hand side of the road for perhaps a mile. A beautiful white bird rises from the swamp and flies away in the direction of the Burundi border. There are surprisingly few sounds, though. An occasional cicada but no birdsong or dogs barking. It is good to stop briefly. With so many bodies around it is dangerous to drink stream water, but there is a nice sound to the water. I let it ripple over my mind and turn my face into the breeze that has come in from the east.

By the time we start up again we agree to keep going until we reach the border. There is no more time left for stopping, unless Edward's car breaks down, of course. Above the bridge we turn right and on to a sandy patch of roadway. On our left there is a steep hillside thickly covered in banana plants and forest. To the right are the swamps. We turn a corner and lying in the roadway are two vehicles. One is a lorry that is wedged into the ditch next to the swamp. A few yards away is a minibus lying on its side. There are two big craters in the road. Both vehicles are badly damaged, but they have not started to rust. Whatever happened here happened fairly recently. Edward is flashing his lights *again. We stop and wait. Glenn appears at the window on Moses's side. 'The road must be mined. We'll have to be fucking careful here. Moses, stay away from the middle of the road, man, try and keep in as far to the hillside as possible. We'll follow in your tracks.' He delivers the advice calmly and walks back to the other car. Landmines! I have seen what they do to cars. A massive boom under your backside and then fire and screaming and death. Ernest shrugs and smiles. 'At least if you die in a landmine you die quickly,' he smirked. At this I want to throttle him. I am scared out of my wits. Here we are on a dirt road in the back end of nowhere with landmines and he wants to make jokes. David taps me on the shoulder and winks. I can tell from his expression that he is worried but he is telling me in his own way to ignore Ernest. Moses starts the car up again and we move forward, slowly turning towards the side of the road and then straightening out. I am sweating and wide awake. I wish I was in the second car. I am convinced our car will hit the mine first. Moses has his eyes glued to the road surface just in front of him. He is watching for any bumps, undulations, anywhere hands might recently have been, sweeping the sand over the mine. Then I see something moving in the road about one hundred yards ahead. My heart leaps against the wall of my chest. 'David, look, look ahead of us,' I shout. There are two men on the road. They are kneeling down, doing something on the road. 'Ernest, look there right in front of us,' shouts David. Moses seems to be in a trance. He cannot take his eyes off the immediate road surface. Ernest grabs his bayonet and quickly fixes it on to the top of his rifle. The sound of steel meeting steel sends a shock wave through Moses. The men in the road see us, jump and dive into the swampland at the side of the road. Ernest is fiddling with the gun. Getting ready to fire. But he can't see the target. David's face has turned completely white. He is talking calmly to Moses. 'Turn the car, Moses, turn around now,' he says. But Moses is looking dumbfounded. I shout at him. 'Turn it, for God's sake, Moses. Get us out of here, there are men on the road. Interahamwe. Get us out of here.' Moses turns the vehicle quickly. A three-hand turn in a matter of seconds. The others do not understand what is happening. I look out the window and gesture frantically to them. I keep expecting to hear a fusillade of shots. Edward turns his car and follows Moses, as we accelerate back along the roadway, past the ruined trucks and across the bridge away from the swampland. I have a St Christopher medal around my neck and I start to kiss it. I pray. God, don't let me die on a roadside here so far from those I love. I don't want to die here. I don't want to die. Get me out of here safely. Please. We cannot be sure if the men had guns. I think I saw at least one rifle. What were they doing in the roadway? I suspect they were laying a mine, preparing an ambush for us. From their position they would have seen our vehicle approaching from a considerable distance. We must have come up on them more quickly than they expected. It is only RPF traffic on the roads now. The men must have thought we were a small rebel patrol. An ambush, I tell myself, they were preparing an ambush. The landmine to immobilize and wound, and then finish us off with guns and knives. Ernest has been shaken out of his torpor. As we speed back along the roadway he is watching the ditches carefully, fingering the stock of his rifle.*

It seems to take an eternity to reach Kabuga again. Here we stop while Ernest goes to tell the local commander that there are Interahamwe active on the road to Burundi. Then Ernest comes back with the cheery news that there are Interahamwe active everywhere in the countryside. 'Well, that's very fucking reassuring,' says Tony. He is angry when he says this but then he begins to laugh. We all join in. Ernest, however, refrains from laughter. He points to his watch. 'Maybe we can still make the border if we try the other route,' he says. We want to get out of Rwanda so badly that we agree.

The next road is much like the first. The sun is starting to set now. It is a beautiful evening but we are too nervous to care. Moses says his stomach is giving him trouble. We stop and he disappears into a deserted hut. Edward climbs underneath the troublesome car and begins tinkering with the metal bolt that has been placed there by the Ethiopian. When Moses reappears I call out to Edward that it's time to get going. But he continues working under the car. 'Come on, Edward. We haven't got time for that,' says Tony. I am starting to worry that we will be stuck in the bush at nightfall. The border is still at least three hours away. Our best hope now is to find a rebel garrison where we can bed down for the night. After calling out twice more to Edward, I finally lose my temper. 'Do you want to fucking die out here? Is that it? Do you want us all to fucking die out here? Get out from there and get in the car and drive. Just drive. Do you understand that?' I scream. Something has been unhinged inside and I am out of control. Fear has taken over. I have been in tight spots before and have never lost my temper. But this is different. There is a vulnerability, a closeness to death, that is stretching my nerves like piano wire. Edward comes out from under the car and gives me a sullen look. He shouts something back but I cannot understand him. We move towards each other aggressively, but Tony stands between us. 'Take it easy, Fergs, take it easy. Remember he's a kid. He's a lot younger than you are. He's full of pride. If you shout at him he'll just retreat from us. We need him on our side. Try and be nice to him.' I shrug and go back to the car, muttering to myself. Moses is sitting with his head on the steering wheel. 'That fellow,' he says, 'he is a troublesome fellow. A very troublesome fellow.'

About half an hour later the road forked in two. One track led south towards Burundi, the other looped back in the direction of Kigali. Driving south, we entered an area of forest. There were no settlements of any kind here. By now the sun had started to slip away across the trees, and David calculated that the dark was less than an hour away. He looked drained and agitated and I imagined he was thinking of his wife and his children. I rolled the window down, hoping that I would hear any shooting or voices more easily that way. There were wood pigeons starting to call in the overhanging trees, and a rich, piny scent was filtering through the odours of dust and sweat in the car. After a long period of scanning the trees my eyes began to hurt. I was seeing nothing but flickering shades of green

and endless dark hollows where tracks ran into the forest. I
lay back and watched the darkening sky through the rear
window of the Land Rover. Edward's car was still making
unhealthy noises but there was no way we could stop now.
If it broke down we would simply have to abandon it and
pack everybody into one vehicle. That would have meant
dumping petrol and equipment but there was unanimity
among the group. We were racing against the night and
needed every single second of daylight.

Emerging from the forest, we came to a stretch of open
savannah and a sign pointing south to the village of Zaza.
'Only two kilometres,' Ernest said cheerily. A short distance further on we came to an RPF checkpoint. The
young soldiers were nervous. They were not used to
vehicles coming through at this hour of the day. I am not
sure but I think I picked up the word 'Interahamwe' in the
conversation between Ernest and his comrades in arms. We
were waved on and about ten minutes later drove into the
village of Zaza. There was a second checkpoint at the
entrance to the village and we were directed to a seminary
where the RPF was guarding several hundred Hutu prisoners. They were dressed in the pink uniforms of common
criminals and most of them were men who had worked on
the body-collecting details during the massacres. Now they
had been captured by the RPF and were waiting while
their fate was decided. They sat in the courtyard of the
seminary singing religious songs. One of them played a
guitar, twangy and out of tune but a sound of sweet

normality after the fear of our journey. The RPF commander was a young man who spoke fluent English and immediately asked me if I could arrange for the BBC to play a request for him. 'Ask them to play Phil Collins, "One More Night". Do you know the song? My name is Celestine. Please get them to play the request. I will listen for it,' he pleaded. Anxious to stay on his right side, I told him that I would do my best. Ernest had once again retreated into silence and was making no attempt to negotiate food and accommodation on our behalf. Thinking we would make Burundi by nightfall, we had neglected to carry food with us on the last leg of the journey. Commander Celestine said he would give us some maize meal and salt. That was all the soldiers had. We could sleep in an old classroom near the main checkpoint leading into the town.

'Are there Interahamwe in the area?' I asked.

'Oh, yes, they are out there. They are living in the woods and the swamps. At night they come back to the abandoned houses and see what they can get to eat. Sometimes they sleep in their old houses, and then at dawn they run away again,' said Celestine. He said his men were mounting regular patrols around the village at night to ward off any attack. With a few hundred Hutu prisoners and only a handful of troops – I counted about fifteen – Commander Celestine was in a very isolated position come nightfall.

★

The parish of Zaza, Commune of Sake. Report of African Rights.

'At least 800 people were killed in a string of massacres in Zaza parish in southern Kibungo during 9–12 of April. Zaza is the site of one of the oldest and most prestigious Roman Catholic missions in Rwanda. The people who fled there doubtless believed that, as one of the places of origin for the Christian religion in Rwanda, it would be a sanctuary.

African Rights visited the parish of Zaza on 29 May and met Beatrice Umamwezi, a survivor of the massacre at Zaza . . .

"The children came out first and had only just reached the door when they started macheting them. When they saw what was happening to their children, the mothers who had tried to get up instinctively fell to the ground. I was underneath one of these women, still naked. The Interahamwe came in and started beheading the women. One of the heads fell on my back. They went around to see if anybody might still be breathing. If they found someone was alive, down came the machete which ended their life. The blood of many of these women was pouring all over me. They could not see me; my head was completely underneath the body of another woman. Since the rest of me was soaked in blood, they thought I was dead. At 7.00 pm the electricity was cut off. I had a wound on the top of my head. A woman had flung a leg on top of me. My head was injured when they hacked off her leg. I looked around and realized I was the only survivor in the dormitory. There had been between forty and fifty people, mainly women and children."'

★

The commander eventually showed us to a small room in a cluster of rooms attached to an abandoned school and dispensary. There were chairs and tables scattered around outside the buildings along with books and pieces of chalk. Ernest found a comic book and sat and read while we cooked the maize. I went around the side of the building to urinate and caught the smell of bodies from the field behind our room. I pulled back but the smell followed me. Two weeks previously I would have gone to see what was lying there. Now I could not bear the thought of looking at another corpse. There was hardly any moonlight and the village seemed swamped by the darkness. There was no movement on the main street and even the soldiers at the checkpoint had stopped their chatter, listening like us to the sounds of the night, afraid of what might lie beyond the perimeter. Was that an animal rustling through the bush? That bird sound – was that not the song of a daytime bird? Why would there be such a call at night? Perhaps it was a signal. But nobody was going out to check on these noises. We were in the small cell of the village with hundreds of Hutu prisoners, a handful of RPF soldiers and the stench of the recently murdered population wafting through the window. Out there in the darkness were the killers. Maybe they had watched us drive into Zaza. They might have been as close as the tree-line at the end of the field behind our room. The incident on the first road left us all badly shaken. Now in Zaza, I was beginning to feel that we would never get out of Rwanda. Although we had planned to leave all our equipment in the cars, Glenn decided to haul out the generator. The light drew squadrons of moths but was a blissful relief from the dark and its endless sounds. The maize meal was sour and stodgy but we chewed on regardless. David made tea and began to talk about the old days of the BBC. It was his way of keeping our minds off the misery of the situation. And then Glenn produced a photograph of his wife and their three dogs. 'I can't wait to see her,' he said, passing the picture around the group of us. In a few minutes we were all passing around photographs of our families, and talking about our lives at home, lives that seemed more precious to us now than we ever could have imagined. I asked Ernest if he had any photographs. 'My family are dead,' he replied. There was an embarrassed silence. Then David stood up and offered Ernest the cup of tea he had been drinking. Ernest smiled and politely refused. Although I had begun to detest Ernest, I now saw that beneath the mask of cynicism and indifference, he was lonely and sad, unable to relate his own loss to journalists who must have seemed like creatures from another planet.

After Glenn had switched off the generator I swallowed a sleeping tablet. I gave one each to Tony and Glenn. David had drifted off the moment his head touched the ground. I was too nervous, and the smell was too wretched, for any more moments of wakefulness than were absolutely necessary. In a few minutes the drug was flowing through my veins, and I fell into a dead, dreamless sleep. Ernest remained upright and awake, watching the door.

The Burundi border, 9 am, 12 June 1994. We are here at last. The last stretch of road was nerve-racking. Ernest said he saw more men in the hills. There was more fixing of bayonets. Near the border we passed several burned-out cars. They probably belonged to Tutsis trying to flee into Burundi. According to Ernest the area that was open and grassy was once one of Habyarimana's favourite hunting grounds. At the RPF post before the border a drunken man came out and started shouting at us. He was a Tutsi survivor and was angry with the international community. It was the first time I had seen anything like indiscipline at an RPF checkpoint. The man wanted to know why we were supporting the Rwandan government. Ernest spoke calmly to the man and quietened him. We were allowed to drive on, a short distance of half a mile to the Burundian customs and immigration. Now we are here waiting to meet Rizu Hamid. She is an African-born Asian who worked with me during the South African elections. Rizu is tough and dedicated and has spent the past few weeks travelling into government territory on our behalf. She is bringing two new vehicles because this is the point where we say goodbye to Moses and Edward. Being Ugandans and according to the Interahamwe 'allies of the RPF', it would be suicidal to take them with us on to the government side. Although it is still early the Burundian policemen and officials are drinking beer. There are several crates stacked around them, and scores of empty bottles. Some of the policemen are bleary-eyed. They must have been going at it all night. They are Tutsis. In Burundi nearly all the soldiers and policemen are from the minority group. Ernest is given a warm welcome and offered a beer, which he declines. The Burundians play cards and chat among themselves, briefly checking our passports before stamping them. A radio is blaring jangly Zairean pop. This party will go on all day. We sit in the shade of a huge tree whose roots stretch across the ground under the customs posts. A few refugees pass by. They are Tutsis on their way back into Rwanda. The border guards don't bother to check them. A Red Cross convoy appears, churning up the dust in clouds, and is waved through. Moses and Edward are anxious to be on their way. If they drive hard they might make the Ugandan border by nightfall. They must go back along the route we have travelled and both are nervous. 'I like travelling with you Mr Fergal. Maybe someday we can meet in Kampala and have some beer and remember this,' Moses says. Edward comes over and shakes my hand. Any ill feeling between us has evaporated. The drivers and Ernest wave goodbye and as they move up the road I notice Moses stopping his car to pick up some refugees who are struggling along in the morning heat. After an hour passes I hear the sound of an engine, and dust starts to rise in the distance. It is Rizu: small with a mop of curly black hair and a broad smile. She stops the car and walks towards us, clutching a bag of food. 'My God, you lot look rough,' she says. But we haven't seen a mirror in weeks. It is not until that night, sitting in a bath in Bujumbura, that I notice the mud caked on to my skin. It has found its way into every nook and cranny of my body. I scrub *hard; it flows off and the warm water turns a dark brown. After a while the water starts to go cold. But I just lie there, drinking and drinking until I am almost too drunk to get up. God, I feel weary and confused. Who am I tonight? Where am I?*

CHAPTER EIGHT

Killers

Rizu walked back to the car accompanied by a young soldier. His name was Patrice and he had been a sergeant in the Rwandan armed forces for the past two years. Patrice had agreed to take us to the outskirts of Butare. There were nearly thirty roadblocks on the fifteen miles of road between Butare and the border post. The Interahamwe manning these posts had been heavily involved in the genocide. They were still on the look-out for Tutsis and were pathologically suspicious of foreigners. With the RPF advancing steadily into the area, the militias and the Rwandan army were in a state of flux, hoping that the rebels would be turned back at Kigali but expecting an invasion at any time. Rizu had already made several journeys up to Butare and had found the experience stressful, to say the least. She was courageous and knew her way around Africa better than most. Rizu had grown up in Tanzania, spoke fluent Swahili (a language widely spoken in parts of Rwanda) and was a skilled negotiator, understanding when to exert pressure and when to appear compliant and humble. Such instinct could mean the difference between life and death on the Rwandan roadblocks. Rizu might have spent much of her adult life in England, but her skill in dealing with the trials of African life was undiminished by the long absence from the continent. Rizu had managed to persuade Patrice that it was in the interests of the Rwandan army to escort us into Butare. She had explained that we wanted to get to the 'other side of the story'. The fact that reporting the 'other side' essentially involved painting a picture of the regime of terror in the government areas and exploring the pathology of genocide was something Rizu had tactfully neglected to mention. Patrice was courteous and neatly dressed and spoke softly and slowly. It was hard to imagine him as a killer. Yet if he was based at the Rwandan border he must have seen the terrible slaughter that had taken place in the area from April onwards. Tutsis attempting to flee into Burundi had been stopped and hacked down as they tried to cross the Kanyaru River near the border. Others had been killed as they attempted to move through the border itself. I wanted to ask Patrice about this but decided to wait until he had seen us safely through the roadblocks.

The road from the border wound through pine-forested hills for several kilometres. There was life here: people in the fields tending crops, small boys herding livestock, smoke rising from the chimneys of huts. The first three roadblocks were easy enough: groups of peasants in ragged clothes sitting around with machetes and clubs. The moment they saw Patrice the men stood up and pushed back the barriers. The barricades were composed of slender young trees that had been chopped down and placed on top of crates and barrels. At the fourth roadblock, on the outskirts of a small village, we decided to stop and try to interview some of the Interahamwe. Patrice walked ahead of us and spoke to a group of men. Children came up to our car and begged for sweets. Tony doled out some toffees and the children grabbed them, running down the road, laughing and cheering. I took out several cartons of cigarettes and walked to where Patrice and the men were standing. In the few minutes since we had stopped the crowd at the barricade had grown bigger. There were more than twenty men, most of them holding machetes or axes or clubs. They had asked Patrice if we were Belgians. Had the answer been yes we would have been killed on the spot. 'The people think the Belgians are the allies of the RPF. They think they are responsible for all the troubles in this country,' explained Patrice. A few weeks before Radio Mille Collines had been broadcasting appeals inciting the peasantry to murder any Belgians they found. The Brussels government had lent its support to the Arusha Peace Accords and refused to sell arms to the Rwandan military. On the other hand French journalists were more than welcome in the government zone. France was an ally and its citizens were to be treated with respect. The vigilantes spoke neither English nor French. We were dependent on Patrice for translations: he would be free to interpret the conversation in whatever way he wished. Yet in the short journey from the border he had come across as fairly naïve. His rationalization of the crisis in the country was simple: this was a war against the RPF and nobody else. He had no problem with individual Tutsis. Some of his relatives were married to Tutsis. There was none of the racist rhetoric that infected the public utterances of the interim government's spokesmen. In any event I had no option but to trust Patrice to translate my questions and their answers honestly.

The men at the barricade looked as if they had not slept in days. Their clothing was either too small or too large, and might well have been stolen from people whose body sizes were vastly different. To my relief there was no smell of alcohol. It was probably too early in the day for that. On the road up to Butare there was a very important rule: never travel late in the afternoon. The later the hour, the greater the chance that men at the roadblocks would be drunk. After a few moments more of softening up from Patrice ('These are journalists from England. They do not mean any harm. You should talk to them. You must explain our side of the story.') the men agreed to be interviewed.

Just as we were about to start filming, a tall man, immaculately dressed in a white shirt with black slacks and well-polished brown shoes, strolled out from a house near the barricade. His name was Louis and he was a refugee from Kigali. He had worked as a civil servant but had been forced to flee when the RPF seized the part of the city he was living in. He had an air of confidence, of education and sophistication, that made the others defer to him. The problem was with the RPF wanting to seize power and set up their own dictatorship, he said. All they wanted was to re-establish the Tutsi aristocracy once more. He wanted me to know that he was an educated man and understood how politics worked. The RPF had been causing trouble since 1990. But what about the killing of Tutsis, I wondered, what did he think of that? Oh, he regretted killing but the whole thing had been started not by the Hutus but by the rebels. A man wearing a peaked cap, who seemed to be the barricade commander, interjected: 'The Tutsis don't want to share this country with another race. They want us to be their slaves again like in the old days.' Another voice spoke up: 'They want to colonize other people. But you must remember, we are human beings too.' These last words struck me as ironic, even sad in a way. The man who spoke them was dressed in rags and was barefoot. He looked frightened and worn out. It was quite possible that he had been involved in the killing. *We are human beings too*. The words of the men at the roadblock were almost word for word a recitation of the government's line. These men really did believe that they were about to be returned to the dark ages of Tutsi autocracy. All the stories of oppression and humiliation that had been handed down from their parents, all the conspiracy theories of the government, and all the fear caused by the RPF incursions since 1990 had been whipped up by extremist politicians to produce a pathological hatred of the Tutsis. I asked one of the men what would happen if a Tutsi came up to the roadblock. He simply smiled. They eventually waved us on our way with handshakes and smiles. I did not know what to feel about them. Revulsion at their warped psychology certainly. But also pity. These were people who lived in wretched poverty, who had been recruited to do the fighting and killing for people who were now safely in exile. Very soon the RPF would come and rout this rabble, either killing them or driving them into exile. The knowledge that they had almost certainly been part of the genocide prevented too deep a sense of pity. But I could not help feeling that they were the lesser part of the evil that had been unleashed.

As we drove further on the atmosphere at the roadblocks became more tense. Men would come running up to the window of the car and demand my identification. They held up machetes; some clutched grenades. The nearer we got to Butare the more sophisticated was the weaponry. Many of them were illiterate. They clutched the passports and made intense examinations of the photographs before handing them back. On the final stretch of road there was an argument with a local gendarme. He was officious and determined to hold us up in order to display his authority to the others on the roadblock.

We were made to get out of the car. The gendarme

could read. As the checking of our details went on, the Interahamwe crowded around us. At least one of them was drunk. 'I want beer. Give me beer,' he demanded. There was some whisky in the car but Glenn warned me not to hand it over. 'Give that to him and we'll never get out of here. They'll rob everything, get pissed and who knows what they'll do,' he said. Instead I handed around some cigarettes. This mollified the drunkard. He was carry-ing two grenades in the belt of his trousers and a long machete. I remembered the stories of what happened to Tutsis at the roadblocks on this road. The singling out, the beating and humiliation and then the killing. Women who were seized at these barricades were frequently raped before being murdered. I knew that somewhere near each of these barriers there was a mass grave, perhaps several graves holding the bodies of the local Tutsi population. The gendarme wanted to know if any of us were Belgians. 'Not at all,' said Rizu. 'British and South African.' Rizu was speaking in Swahili to the gendarme. She was patient. She laughed and joked with him. She let him understand that she accepted his power. We were not a threat to his safety or his ego. The slow palaver worked and we were allowed to move on. At every roadblock from now on the same wheeling and dealing had to be repeated. Rizu never lost her calm. I was awestruck by her capacity for quietening the rowdiest and most terrifying-looking characters.

Closer to Butare the road passed along the edge of a

deep ravine. From here it was possible to look out across row upon row of terraced hills, across pockets of mist gathered in small valleys, and over the streams and rivers that denoted the boundary with Burundi. To a fleeing Tutsi this sight must have represented a vision of hope, however transitory. From the ravine's edge they would have speculated on whether it was safer to cross the open countryside or to keep moving along the roadway, ducking into the bush when they came within view of the roadblocks. Either way they must have sensed that their chances were slim and that Burundi, though physically close, was still dangerously distant. With the majority of the population out hunting for them, in a country as small as Rwanda there were few places for the Tutsis to hide. I found the roadblocks truly frightening.

At the main barricade on the outskirts of Butare, David spoke to one of the Interahamwe leaders, a man named Jacques. He was an educated man, another former civil servant who came from Butare. Glenn filmed him frisking people at the roadblock, roughly grabbing men between the legs, pulling their shirts back and forth to see if they had recently been carrying military packs, checking their legs for signs of bootmarks. Women were treated only marginally better. The ID cards were checked most rigorously of all. They were looking out for forgeries, for people who had managed to secure cards that changed their identity from Tutsi to Hutu. Families were made to unpack their baggage. It did not matter that it might have taken all morning to wrap and tie everything together into manageable bundles. Jacques really enjoyed his work.

'What are you doing?' asked David.

'We are looking for combatants,' replied Jacques.

'Who are the combatants?'

'The RPF of course,' he replied, grabbing the genitals of a retarded boy who had come smiling up to the road-block with a bag of sweets. The boy just stood smiling as Jacques squeezed his body from top to bottom.

'But where are the RPF?' David continued.

'The RPF can be the man, the woman, even the child,' said Jacques. He rummaged in the packet of sweets and then pushed the boy away.

'And what do you do when you find them?'

'We hand them over to the authorities . . . they do what they want with them.' He smiled the 'smile'.

Jacques was not being strictly honest and he didn't really care if we knew. The sinister little smile was his way of letting us know what we of course already knew. Tutsis were dead the minute Jacques uncovered their identity. He was the authority, just as every wild-eyed peasant between there and the border now had the power of judge, jury and executioner over the 'enemies of the state'.

Butare itself was crowded with soldiers and Hutu refu-gees. While the city had become a place of terror for Tutsis, Hutus were flocking there to escape the RPF advance. Rizu had made arrangements for us to stay in the city's last functioning hotel. It was owned by the rector of

the University of Butare, whose vast extended family had
arrived from all over Rwanda and colonized the building.
The main gate was guarded by a corporal from the presidential guard. Just across the road, within easy view from our
bedroom windows, was a roadblock commanded by a
particularly officious militiaman. He seemed to constantly
move and shout orders to the other Interahamwe, who
were more inclined to lie in the shade waiting for traffic or
refugees to happen along. Even military cars were stopped
at the roadblock and questioned. Our accommodation was
bare, concrete floors and peeling paint, more like a military
barracks than a hotel. But there were beds and there was
water and the rector's wife sold beer to supplement the
hotel's income. The rector's grandchildren, numerous little
girls and a spoiled boy of about six, careened up and down
the hallways, screaming and laughing excitedly. Under
normal circumstances I would have played with them,
encouraged their games. But the trip from the border had
been too unnerving. I wanted to scream at the children. I
wanted them to shut up. I needed silence for a little while
and a stiff drink. Eventually the children were rounded up
by their respective mothers and sent to bed. The building
became quiet. Outside the traffic on the road had dwindled
away. Now only an occasional army jeep passed by.
Civilians had disappeared altogether. Our room had a
balcony that faced in the direction of the university. This
was Rwanda's premier place of third-level education. Like
every other government-run institute in the country, the

university discriminated severely against Tutsis. Most of the senior academic posts were stuffed with supporters of Habyarimana and the MRND. Once the killings started the university closed down. But the rector and vice-rector retained their chauffeur-driven cars. That night the two men knocked on our bedroom door and asked us if we would like to have a drink and talk.

Of the two, the vice-rector, Dr J. Birchmans Nshimyumuremyi, is the most voluble. They sit directly opposite David and me. It is a beautiful evening. The sun is dipping below the thick garden of trees that surrounds the university. Long, slanting rays of golden light come through the window, illuminating the round face of Mr Birchmans and the full glass of whisky he holds in his chubby fingers. Birchmans is a fat man. He has a moon face and big eyes that bulge when he makes one of his frequent denunciations of the RPF. The rector, on the other hand, is inclined to say little. I sense that he is worried. He asks us for news of the war. Are the rebels near by? he inquires. The rector is already thinking to himself that he must make plans to evacuate his family. He is shocked by the deterioration of the city. It is jammed with strangers. Many of his colleagues have already moved out, heading in the direction of Zaire. This was not how it was supposed to be. The government radio tells him that the defeats are only minor setbacks. How was it one of the presenters described it, 'Like letting in a few goals but with the match still to play for!' Birchmans is worried too but determined not to show it. He slurps the whisky. David and I take turns in questioning the men. David's manner is soothing. His tone is that of a perplexed bystander. I can tell that his maturity and calm impress the rector. David never betrays what he is feeling. Birchmans repeats the line about it all being the fault of the RPF. I let him ramble on about this. The rector supports him but without much enthusiasm. What about the Interahamwe? I ask. Birchmans says they are patriotic young men. They gather together for cultural purposes. I remember now, aeons ago, the young guide who had directed us to Sylvestre Gacumbitsi back in Tanzania had said the Interahamwe were people who organized dances.

I fill the glasses again and ask Birchmans what has happened to the Tutsis who lived in Butare. They have all left, he says. But surely he must have known about the massacres? No, he has seen nothing like that. Yes, he knows that people have been killed, but in a war people are killed.

We are in complete darkness now and David lights a candle. There is an intimacy now which I find deeply uncomfortable. Birchmans's face seems to swell as he rants on about the RPF and how they killed the president in order to provoke the Hutus and start a civil war. This man is probably the second-most prominent academic in Rwanda. He has studied in Belgium and Canada. His English and French are impeccable and he wears spotlessly clean clothes. Yet he struggles to hide his hatred of the Tutsis. He is much too clever to blurt out his feelings, the way the men on the roadblock did. Instead he says that Tutsis inside the country co-operated with the RPF. They helped them invade. As long as he has known them this is the feeling he has had. They were not loyal to the government.

'But did the Tutsis deserve to die?'

'Let me answer your question with a question,' he says.

'No, answer my question first.'

'OK. Did the people killed by the RPF deserve to die?'

'That is a question to be put to the RPF. I am talking to you as a representative of the government and I want you to answer the question. Did they deserve to be killed?'

He pauses. He exhales. 'Killing is a terrible thing, but in war people are killed. That is how it happens.'

I almost expect to hear him say, 'Well, they were asking for it, weren't they?' But Mr Birchmans is far too sophisticated for that. He is a man of such cleverness that he has contrived not to see any of the tens of thousands who have been killed in and around Butare. Nor has he heard any screams of dying people. But he is wondering now what will happen. The people of Rwanda will never accept the RPF as their government. He wants us to understand this very clearly. The Hutus will never again accept being ruled by the Tutsis, who treated them as slaves. The rector listens to Birchmans, nodding his head occasionally. It is only at the end, when they are getting up to go, that he speaks. Again he asks if we know how near the RPF are. Some people in the town have told him that they can hear explosions. He is listening for them, but so far there is nothing.

The following night the rector comes again to our door. 'Come with me,' he says. 'You are Irish, are you not?'

'Yes, I am,' I reply.

'You will like this, then,' he says, opening the door to his *sitting-room, where his wife and several children of all ages are sitting in front of a large television screen. The reception is hazy but I can easily make out the green of the Irish football jerseys. I had forgotten that on the other side of the world, in the middle of the American summer, men were playing in the World Cup. 'Rwanda has no team in this tournament so we will cheer for you,' says the rector.*

I am given the most comfortable seat in the room. A deep leather armchair. I notice several family photographs on the wall. There is a portrait of the rector in his university regalia, and there is the ubiquitous photograph of the Pope. When Ireland score the room explodes into wild cheering. I smile inanely and express my gratitude. While I am sitting watching the game, in a town that has become a citadel of killers, there are thousands of my fellow countrymen cheering and drinking the night away in New York. I wish I was there. I wish I was anywhere but here. 'Goodnight, Monsieur Rector, but you will understand. I have a headache. I am not well and must sleep.' He gives me a puzzled look. There is an element of hurt in his expression. The rector cannot understand why I would reject the friendship of his family. But he says nothing about it. He only shrugs and bids me goodnight.

Most of our time in Butare was spent talking to the Interahamwe on the roadblocks. They spoke incessantly of the Tutsi plot to reimpose feudalism. After a while I ceased to hear them. The camera recorded but the words were old and stale, a script written by the architects of the genocide and repeated endlessly down the line to the most impoverished, illiterate peasant. As the days progressed the militia became more suspicious of our presence. It was now possible to hear RPF shells in the distance. The atmosphere in Butare was becoming paranoid. The town had started out as one of the less dangerous places for Tutsis. That was largely due to the efforts of Jean Habyarimana, the Tutsi préfet of Butare, who had persuaded the military to protect refugees. But Habyarimana was removed from office on 12 April and 'disappeared', presumed murdered. On the day he was ousted and a new préfet appointed the pogroms began. Now all that could be seen of the Tutsis who had crowded into Butare in their tens of thousands was a small group of perhaps 500 who sat outside the municipal offices, awaiting their fate. They dared not move out of the square. There had already been several attacks on people who went to fetch water. The refugees were crammed into a space roughly one quarter the size of a soccer pitch. Their babies cried constantly and they smelt of damp and smoke and excrement. They had no weapons and few possessions. For the time being their safety seemed to be guaranteed by the man who had replaced Habyarimana, Sylvan Nsabimana. When we went to see him, Nsabimana was quite willing to talk. He was a small, fat man who wore a bright Hawaiian shirt and waddled rather than walked. His office was located directly next to a military camp. The soldiers eyed us warily as we got out of the car. David and I went alone into the office while the others stayed with the equipment. In a town swollen with refugees it would have been foolish to leave any valuables unattended.

Nsabimana welcomed us and wanted to know what he could do to help. 'We need a *laissez-passer* to move around,' explained David. 'That should not be a problem. It is good that you come here' the préfet responded.

We told Nsabimana that we needed to talk to him. Why was he giving protection to the Tutsis on the square outside? Before he could answer a tall, thin man stormed into the room. He was smartly dressed in what seemed to be the regulation outfit of the regime's senior men – crisp white shirt and dark slacks – and Nsabimana stiffened when he appeared. Although he spoke in Kinyarwanda it was easy enough to decode his message. What are they doing here? What are you doing talking to them? What are you telling them? The préfet mumbled a response and the tall man sat down, folding his legs and leaning back into the armchair. I noticed that his eyes were heavily bloodshot. He spoke to David in French. What were we doing here?

David explained about our desire to have an official pass that would let us through the roadblocks to film un-hindered. We also needed to talk to the préfet about what was happening in Butare. The tall man wanted to see our identification. We showed him our passports and press cards. Another man, smaller and sleepy-faced, poked his head around the door. The préfet beckoned to him to sit down. The tall one was struggling to keep his loathing of us under wraps. He knew all about the foreign media and all the things they were saying about the Hutus. He was a senior adviser to the government and had heard the lies that were being reported. Nsabimana remained quiet throughout the ranting of his superior. The tall man was clearly the boss. There was going to be no co-operation. It would have to be approved by the government. The situation was too dangerous at the moment. In any case the BBC did nothing but tell lies about Rwanda. It supported the RPF. He wanted us to leave. I could only presume that our presence was not in keeping with his plans for the remaining Tutsis. Whatever was being planned for them was going to happen away from the eyes of the world. Nsabimana began to speak on our behalf. He was sure we had not come to cause harm. There could hardly be any problem with giving us permission to film in the area. There was a derisive snort from the armchair. And then the telephone rang in the room next door. The small man jumped up and ran into the other room. There was a call for the tall man. He left us for several minutes and then returned with an anxious expression on his face. The arrogance had been replaced by uncertainty. There had been some important news from the government. I wondered if he had been told to evacuate, that the rebels were close by. He muttered something about coming back later and then stormed out the door. After he had been gone for a few seconds Nsabimana signed a *laissez-passer* and told the small man to accompany us. 'If there are problems at roadblocks you must explain that they have my permission to be here,' he said.

'What about the Tutsis outside? I have a bad feeling that by the time our programme gets shown those people will be dead,' I said.

'No, I do not think they will be killed. They have no guarantees. But they will not be killed,' he answered. There had been some of the worst massacres in Rwanda in the period since Sylvan Nsabimana took office. Everywhere else in the country the local mayors and préfets had been up to their necks in the killing. Why should he be different? I had no answer to that question, and in that time and place there was no way of finding out quickly. Nsabimana said the killing was being done by hotheads. Not all the Hutus were like that. In fact the following day he was going to try and help evacuate several hundred Tutsi orphans from Butare. Even now he was negotiating with the army for an escort to the border. A Swiss aid group had gathered the children together. Some were injured, others were traumatized. By tomorrow night hopefully they would be in Burundi. David asked if we could accompany the convoy. Nsabimana thought for a second and then said that it would be fine with him. He would ensure we had no trouble with the roadblock. We made an arrangement to meet the préfet the following day at a local park where the evacuation was going to start. That night, when we went back to film the refugees outside the préfet's office, the army sent us away. The area had been closed off for the night for security reasons. The soldiers on guard told us to go home. If we stayed any longer we would be breaking the curfew.

From the roadway it sounds like the chattering of little birds. There are many, many small voices, all of them babbling excitedly. In the park children from the age of two upwards are being organized into groups with numbers pinned to their clothes. The clothing is bright and new. Several aid workers go around reassuring the infants who are crying. People are very tense. On one recent convoy the Interahamwe seized several children from a truck and killed them. After all, the militiamen have been told not to repeat the mistake of 1959. Tutsi orphans are a prime target. Nsabimana arrives with an army officer and a civilian official. There is much toing and froing with the aid workers. Nsabimana goes to each of the three trucks and speaks to the children in Kinyarwanda.

David, Glenn and Tony climb into the lead lorry, and Rizu and I follow in the Land Rover. We are at the rear of the convoy. 'Stay close to them. We don't want to get separated,' I say. 'I think I am able to drive, thank-you,' she replies tartly. I apologize immediately. It is just my nervousness at the thought of those thirty roadblocks between Butare and the border. Even with Nsabimana there is no guarantee that the militia will wave the children through. Before we leave the doors of the trucks are partially closed. There is a sufficient gap to a-llow air in. Inside the children continue to talk to each other.

I look inside the first truck and in the semi-dark see the wide eyes of the infants staring back at me. They are quiet for a few minutes, until I take my head away and the excited chatter begins again. The aid workers climb into the trucks. There is a Japanese photographer with them and he begins to sing nursery rhymes, encouraging the children to join in. With the voices high above the grumble of the trucks we head out on to the road and south towards Burundi.

Nsabimana's limousine moves in between the trucks, racing ahead every time we approach a roadblock. Rizu keeps the car almost glued to the last truck. We say very little to each other. The journey is too tense for conversation. All of our energy and will seems directed to the task of getting to the border without an incident. I wonder what we will do if they try and seize some children. The militia would kill us if we tried to intervene. But could we stand by and watch little innocents being dragged off to be butchered? Roadblock after roadblock. The same routine each time. Nsabimana stops, rolls down his window and begins the explanation. The sight of the army officer in his car placates the Interahamwe. But my heart stops when we reach the roadblock where the gendarme had interrogated us a few days previously. The men at this barrier are more numerous and well armed than any of the rest. Nsabimana's car stops. The trucks grind to a halt. From the front seat of the car I can see Glenn's blond head bobbing around near the door of the last truck. The Japanese photographer is sitting there as well talking to the children. A militiaman with a machete approaches the truck slowly. He walks around to the back door. Another man carrying a club joins him. There is sweat pouring down my forehead. Rizu coughs and taps her fingers on the steering wheel. The militiamen gaze into the truck, one after the other. Seconds stretch tortuously into minutes. Other Interahamwe are moving around the first and second trucks. Nsabimana is still talking. Then his hand appears out of the window of the car. He is waving us forward and the convoy starts up and once more rolls south. By the time we reach the border post both Rizu and I are beyond the stage of worry. I believe we have reached a stage of acceptance that allows us to move beyond fear and simply exist without thinking.

At the border Patrice is waiting with several other soldiers. He welcomes us like old friends and then goes to help with the lifting of the children down from the trucks. The children follow the instructions of the aid workers without complaint. Some of them slip into the bushes to answer the call of nature and then run back to their preassigned groups. The préfet is talking to the border guards, showing them his piece of paper and then sitting down to chat for a few minutes. When he comes back I ask him why he was willing to help the children.

'They should not be blamed for the problems of the adult world. I have my own children. I would not want to see this happening to them. A child is innocent. It has no say in what happens,' he says. (Sylvan Nsabimana does not know that soon after he left for the border the military commander of Butare issued an instruction for his dismissal. Nsabimana was replaced by an army officer.) As we talk the procession of children moves towards the border. The older ones are holding

ing the hands of the smaller ones. The aid workers carry the babies. They pause momentarily at the barrier, dip underneath, straightening up for their last footsteps out of Rwanda, and then walking quietly together up the road to Burundi. Somewhere behind them, lying in mass graves or pit latrines or burned-out houses, were the bodies of their parents. As I watch them enter Burundi and board the buses that have been lined up to take them to Bujumbura, I think of Frank Ndore and how he made the same journey back in 1959. I wish for all the world that he could be here, that he could greet these exiles and guide them away from the past. Right now I suppose Frank is with the RPF forces advancing on the remnants of government army. Frank and Valence are out there on the other side of the line. In a few weeks they will be in Butare. The town will have fallen easily. The rector and the vice-rector and all of Butare's Hutu elite will be gone along with the soldiers and the militiamen. The majority will head for Zaire, where Mobutu has offered sanctuary. Some will head for the 'safe area' established by the French near the Zairean border. And when the French leave, having staved off a final rebel victory by a few months, the fleeing Hutus will move to Goma, where the genocidal regime has set up its headquarters in exile. Sylvan Nsabimana will flee to Nairobi and will find his name appearing in a list of people accused of complicity in the genocide. It is true that his period as préfet saw massive killings in the Butare region. He protests his innocence.

For now it is good enough to be leaving. This departure is like a benediction. Uplifting. I feel as if I am escaping from prison. I know the others feel exactly the same way. Glenn and

Tony are joking and laughing. Rizu is talking about the meal we will have in Nairobi. And David, as ever, is guiding us along. He is jotting down 'things to do' in his notebook and planning the editing of the film. At the Burundian passport control we sip warm beer. Glenn talks about the fish he is going to catch once he gets back to South Africa. Tony has plans to visit Japan with his wife. Rizu is making a feature film in Zimbabwe. Not even the Burundian customs forcing us to unload all of our equipment can take away the sweet feeling of release. Rwanda is now the country behind us. It no longer lies down the road, a slowly unfolding nightmare. Our journey home has begun. It is impossible to tell you how good it feels.

EPILOGUE

Blood Following

It is one year since I travelled through Rwanda. Although I live in Asia now, the memories of that time remain as vivid as if the experiences had occurred only days ago. This recall extends beyond the photographic images etched into my mind. I can still smell the smells, hear the voices. I can still feel the tightening in my stomach when I remember the empty bush tracks and the night coming on. Glenn and David have both been back to Rwanda. I was asked to go when the cholera epidemic struck the camps in July 1994, but I declined. It was too soon after the last journey. There were bad dreams to deal with and a deep sense of weariness with Africa. I think I would like to go back someday. I want to meet Frank again and I want to travel the roads that once held such fear for me. What I know about Rwanda these days is largely gleaned from the newspapers and the radio. But these are uncertain sources. As before, the international media's attention is still largely focused on the situation in the refugee camps and not with the slow, painful process of rebuilding a country out of the ashes of genocide. The process of bringing the killers to justice has begun. But those imprisoned inside Rwanda itself are the minnows. The principal architects of the killing are sitting in Zaire and Tanzania. President Mobutu Sese Seko, arguably the most corrupt leader in the world, has provided a safe haven, presumably in the hope that the extremists will one day soon take power again in Rwanda. The defeated Rwandan army is waiting in camps along the Zairean border, intimidating and murdering refugees who attempt to return home, convincing others that they will be massacred by the RPF. Just as the world lacked the will to stop the slaughter when it could, so it also lacks the determination to pressurize Mobutu so that the genocidal politicians and soldiers are denied protection. The French-based group Médecins Sans Frontières rightly describe the camps as 'humanitarian havens' for the killers.

The RPF is struggling to govern a country with the vast majority of its population either in exile or inclined to regard the organization as the old Tutsi aristocracy in a new guise. In its attempts to disband the camps inside Rwanda that have become breeding grounds for the extremist cause, the RPF has used a brutality that simply reinforces the fears of Hutu peasants fed on a diet of anti-Tutsi propaganda. Reports of killings of several hundred Hutu civilians by the RPF shortly after they took power have helped to deepen the mistrust. Similarly conditions in its prisons are a cause for deep concern. The deaths of prisoners from overcrowding cannot be simply explained away as the inevitable consequence of the war's chaotic aftermath. A number of human rights organizations have claimed that their attempts to investigate excesses by the RPF have been obstructed by the military. In saying this, however, one must be careful not to suggest any equality of responsibility between the RPF troops and the Interahamwe militiamen and Rwandan soldiers who carried out the genocide. There is none, either in terms of scale or intent. The RPF and its allies in the government of national unity do seem to be genuinely concerned with creating a country in which massacre politics become a thing of the past. Unlike the regimes that governed Rwanda since independence, the RPF-led government has not, thus far, sunk into a mire of corruption, clientelism and cynical ethnic politics. Its leaders model themselves on Uganda's Yoweri Museveni, a man with puritan standards of personal honesty. Whatever their faults, the RPF and the moderate Hutu politicians who survived the genocide remain the best chance for Rwanda. The alternative is a return of the butchers. To those who argue that there should be a compromise with the extremists, an agreement to drop war crimes charges in the interests of reconciliation, I say think again. These are people who have shown not a single shred of remorse, who have either lied about what happened or who have boasted of their part in it. What is more important is the realization that they would do the same again given the slightest chance. They are not interested in reconciliation. The propaganda and hatred that spawned the genocide are being spewed out to the refugees in Zaire and Tanzania every day.

I am a passionate believer in democracy but am forced to accept that it is not a viable option in Rwanda for the foreseeable future. An open election in which the extremists were allowed to stand would probably see a return to power of the MRND and a re-establishment of the corrupt rule of pre-genocide Rwanda. The RPF-led government would be guaranteed the support of perhaps 10 to 15 per cent of the population – in other words what remains of the Tutsis and the moderate Hutus. Even though there is evidence that many ordinary Hutus either rejected the campaign of genocide or had to be forced to take part in it, it would be unrealistic to imagine that they would cast a vote for an organization that has been so successfully demonized by the extremists. It may take many long years before Rwanda can contemplate a free election. In its place there must be an attempt by the RPF to broaden its own political base and to construct a representative coalition with respect for the rule of law. The number of Hutus in the organization is still dismally few. To argue, as the RPF does, that ethnic identity should not matter is to miss the point. In Rwanda the labels 'Hutu' and 'Tutsi' are going to remain part of the political reality for some time to come. There were rebel commanders whom I met who recognized this and spoke of the need to attract 'moderate' Hutus. That task has been made immeasurably more difficult due to the murder of numerous Hutu opposition figures by the presidential guard in the early days of the genocide. Yet those Hutu politicians who survived the genocide, whom I met in Byumbe and Kigali, were as adamant as the RPF that, given time, a Rwanda free of hatred could be created. Such determination was heartening coming from men who had lost most of their families and political associates. Only time will tell whether Rwandan politics can be de-ethnicized to a degree that makes democracy meaningful and secure.

It is likely that the defeated army will try at some stage to reinvade Rwanda. The presidential guard is still intact and the Interahamwe continues to train and rearm. If there is such an invasion one can only hope that it will be beaten back and a decisive, final defeat inflicted on the extremists. Perhaps only then will the large population of Hutu refugees, held in thrall by the propaganda and brutality of the Rwandan army and militias, be able to contemplate a return to Rwanda. The military threat along the border with Zaire is a powerful impediment to the democratization of Rwanda. While such a threat remains the government in Kigali will feel itself justified in preserving what amounts to a state of emergency in the country. This will continue to have a severely negative effect on human rights.

As for the international community that failed Rwanda so dismally in the months of April and May, it is time to support the new government. Only with well-targeted and supervised aid and advice can the world earn the moral right to influence Rwanda's new rulers for the good. Having done virtually nothing to stop one of the worst acts of mass murder in recent history, the United States, the European Community and the UN must assist the Kigali government. In doing so, the international community will be able to make up for the shameful abandonment of the past, and bring pressure to bear on the new rulers to respect human rights and the rule of law. Neither must there be any doubt, ever, that what happened in Rwanda *was* genocide. The old clichés about 'tribal hatred' are an insult to the dead.

So much for the politics. In personal terms Rwanda, as I mentioned at the outset, continues to exercise a formidable hold on my consciousness. It was unlike any other event I have reported on and in different ways it changed everybody – the survivors most of all, but also the doctors, the aid workers, the priests, the journalists. We had learned something about the soul of man that would leave us with nightmares long into the future. This was not death as I had seen it South Africa, or Eritrea, or Northern Ireland. Nothing could have prepared me for the scale of what I witnessed. It is this immensity of evil that prompts me to speak of the 'soul of man'. I am not an especially religious person but I went to Rwanda believing in a spiritual world in which evil was kept at bay by a powerful force for good. Sometimes the battle was close but I felt there was enough decency and love around to nourish the gift of hope. There will be many who say that I was foolish, naïve to ever have had such faith in man. Maybe they are right. In any event after Rwanda I lost that optimism. I am not sure that it will ever return. For now I can only promise to remember the victims: the dead of Nyarubuye, the wounded and the traumatized, the orphans and the refugees, all of the lost ones whose hands reach out through the ever lengthening distance. At the very outset I asked what it was that dreams asked of us. Perhaps they request something very ordinary: simply that we do not forget.

Hong Kong, June 1995

A Chronology of Genocide

1918: Under the Treaty of Versailles the former German colony of Ruanda-Urundi is made a UN protectorate to be governed by Belgium, adding to the vast Belgian possessions in the Congo. The two territories (later to become Rwanda and Burundi) are administered separately under two different Tutsi monarchs.

1926: Belgians introduce a system of ethnic identity cards differentiating Hutus from Tutsis.

1933: A census of the Rwandan population is carried out by the colonial authorities. Mandatory identity cards stating the ethnic identity of the bearer are extended.

1957: PARMEHUTU (Party for the Emancipation of the Hutus) is formed while Rwanda is still under Belgian rule.

1959: The Tutsi king, Mwaami Rudahigwa, dies. Hutus rise up against the Tutsi nobility and kill thousands. Many more flee to Uganda, Tanzania, Burundi and Zaire.

1962: Rwanda gains independence from Belgium. Wide-scale killing of Tutsis and further massive outflow of refugees, many to Uganda.

Hutu nationalist government of Grégoire Kayibanda's PARMEHUTU comes to power.

1963: Further massacres of Tutsis, this time in response to military attack by exiled Tutsis in Burundi. Again more refugees leave the country. It is estimated that by the mid 1960s half of the Tutsi population is living outside Rwanda.

1967: Renewed massacres of Tutsis.

1973: Purge of Tutsis from universities. Fresh outbreak of killings, again directed at Tutsi community.

The chief of staff of the army, General Juvénal Habyarimana, seizes power, pledging to restore order. He sets up a one-party state. A policy of ethnic quotas is entrenched in all public service employment. Tutsis are restricted to 9 per cent of available jobs.

1975: Habyarimana's political party, the National Revolutionary Movement for Development (Mouvement Révolutionnaire National pour le Développement, or MRND) is formed. Hutus from the president's home area of northern Rwanda are given overwhelming preference in public service and military jobs. This pattern and the exclusion of the Tutsis continues throughout the seventies and eighties.

1986: In Uganda Rwandan exiles are among the victorious troops of Yoweri Museveni's National Resistance Army who take power, overthrowing the dictator Milton Obote. The exiles then form the Rwandan Patriotic Front (RPF), a Tutsi-dominated organization.

1989: The coffee price collapses, causing severe economic hardship in Rwanda.

July 1990: Under pressure from western aid donors Habyarimana concedes the principle of multi-party democracy.

October 1990: Guerrillas of the recently formed RPF

invade Rwanda from Uganda. After fierce fighting in which French and Zairean troops are called in to assist the government, a ceasefire is signed on 29 March 1991.

1990/91: The Rwandan army begins to train and arm civilian militias known as Interahamwe ('Those who stand together'). For the next three years Habyarimana stalls on the establishment of a genuine multi-party system with power-sharing. Throughout this period thousands of Tutsis are killed in separate massacres around the country. Opposition politicians and newspapers are persecuted.

November 1992: Prominent Hutu activist Dr Leon Mugusera appeals to Hutus to send the Tutsis 'back to the Ethiopia' via the rivers.

February 1993: The RPF launches a fresh offensive. The guerrillas reach the outskirts of Kigali and French forces are again called in to help the government side. Fighting continues for several months.

August 1993: At Arusha in Tanzania, following months of negotiations, Habyarimana agrees to power-sharing with the Hutu opposition and the RPF. He also agrees to integrate the RPF into a new Rwandan army, giving the guerrillas almost half the positions among officers and men. The presidential guard was to be merged with elite RPF troops into a smaller republican guard. 2,500 UN troops are subsequently deployed in Kigali to oversee the implementation of the accord.

September 1993–March 1994: President Habyarimana

stalls on setting up of power-sharing government. Training of militias intensifies. Extremist radio station, Radio Mille Collines, begins broadcasting exhortations to attack the Tutsis. Human rights groups warn the international community of impending calamity.

March 1994: Many Rwandan human rights activists evacuate their families from Kigali, believing massacres are imminent.

6 April 1994: President Habyarimana and the president of Burundi, Cyprien Ntaryamira, are killed when Habyarimana's plane is shot down as it comes in to land at Kigali Airport. Extremists, suspecting that the president is finally about to implement the Arusha Peace Accords, are believed to be behind the attack. That night the killing begins.

7 April 1994: The Rwandan armed forces and the Interahamwe set up roadblocks and go from house to house killing Tutsis and moderate Hutu politicians. Thousands die on the first day. UN forces stand by while the slaughter goes on. They are forbidden to intervene, as this would breach their 'monitoring' mandate.

8 April 1994: The RPF launches a major offensive to end the genocide and rescue 600 of its troops surrounded in Kigali. The troops had been based in the city as part of the Arusha Accords.

21 April 1994: The UN cuts the level of its forces from 2,500 to 250 following the murder of ten Belgian soldiers assigned to guard the moderate Hutu prime minister, Agathe Uwiliyingimana. The prime minister is killed and the Belgians are disarmed, tortured and shot and hacked to death. They had been told not to resist violently by the UN force commander, as this would have breached their mandate.

30 April 1994: The UN Security Council spends eight hours discussing the Rwandan crisis. The resolution condemning the killing omits the word 'genocide'. Had the term been used, the UN would have been legally obliged to act to 'prevent and punish' the perpetrators. Meanwhile, tens of thousands of refugees flee into Tanzania, Burundi and Zaire. In one day 250,000 Rwandans, mainly Hutus fleeing the advance of the RPF, cross the border into Tanzania.

17 May 1994: As the slaughter of the Tutsis continues the UN finally agrees to send 6,800 troops and policemen to Rwanda with powers to defend civilians. A fresh Security Council resolution says 'acts of genocide may have been committed'. The United States government forbids its spokespersons to use the word 'genocide'. Deployment of the mainly African UN forces is delayed because of arguments over who will pay the bill and provide the equipment. The United States argues with the UN over the cost of providing heavy armoured vehicles for the peacekeeping forces.

22 June 1994: With still no sign of UN deployment, the Security Council authorizes the deployment of French forces in south-west Rwanda. They create a 'safe area' in territory controlled by the government. Killings of Tutsis continue in the 'safe area', although some are protected by the French. The United States government eventually uses the word 'genocide'.

July 1994: The final defeat of the Rwandan army. The government flees to Zaire, followed by a human tide of refugees. The French end their mission and are replaced by Ethiopian UN troops. The RPF sets up an interim government of national unity in Kigali. A cholera epidemic sweeps the refugee camps in Zaire, killing thousands. Different UN agencies clash over reports that RPF troops have carried out a series of reprisal killings in Rwanda. Several hundred civilians are said to have been executed. Meanwhile the killing of Tutsis continues in refugee camps.

READ MORE IN PENGUIN

In every corner of the world, on every subject under the sun, Penguin represents quality and variety – the very best in publishing today.

For complete information about books available from Penguin – including Puffins, Penguin Classics and Arkana – and how to order them, write to us at the appropriate address below. Please note that for copyright reasons the selection of books varies from country to country.

In the United Kingdom: Please write to *Dept. EP, Penguin Books Ltd, Bath Road, Harmondsworth, West Drayton, Middlesex UB7 0DA*

In the United States: Please write to *Consumer Sales, Penguin USA, P.O. Box 999, Dept. 17109, Bergenfield, New Jersey 07621-0120.* VISA and MasterCard holders call 1-800-253-6476 to order Penguin titles

In Canada: Please write to *Penguin Books Canada Ltd, 10 Alcorn Avenue, Suite 300, Toronto, Ontario M4V 3B2*

In Australia: Please write to *Penguin Books Australia Ltd, P.O. Box 257, Ringwood, Victoria 3134*

In New Zealand: Please write to *Penguin Books (NZ) Ltd, Private Bag 102902, North Shore Mail Centre, Auckland 10*

In India: Please write to *Penguin Books India Pvt Ltd, 706 Eros Apartments, 56 Nehru Place, New Delhi 110 019*

In the Netherlands: Please write to *Penguin Books Netherlands bv, Postbus 3507, NL-1001 AH Amsterdam*

In Germany: Please write to *Penguin Books Deutschland GmbH, Metzlerstrasse 26, 60594 Frankfurt am Main*

In Spain: Please write to *Penguin Books S. A., Bravo Murillo 19, 1° B, 28015 Madrid*

In Italy: Please write to *Penguin Italia s.r.l., Via Felice Casati 20, I–20124 Milano*

In France: Please write to *Penguin France S. A., 17 rue Lejeune, F–31000 Toulouse*

In Japan: Please write to *Penguin Books Japan, Ishikiribashi Building, 2–5–4, Suido, Bunkyo-ku, Tokyo 112*

In Greece: Please write to *Penguin Hellas Ltd, Dimocritou 3, GR–106 71 Athens*

In South Africa: Please write to *Longman Penguin Southern Africa (Pty) Ltd, Private Bag X08, Bertsham 2013*

BY THE SAME AUTHOR

The Bondage of Fear

'An important source for anyone trying to understand how South Africa achieved its transfer of power' – Anthony Sampson in the *Independent*

'Thoughtful, compassionate, shrewd and superbly crafted – a model of judiciously selected episodes and of succinct but never over-simplified explanations of subtleties that need to be understood by anyone interested in the multiple challenges facing the new South Africa. *The Bondage of Fear* is also an adventure story: an adventure story of the spirit' – Dervla Murphy in the *Spectator*

'A first-class journalistic account ... likely to be the most memorable account of this terrible, uplifting time' – John Simpson in the *Literary Review*

'It is Keane's willingness to record his innermost feelings that makes his book so powerful ... This is a moving description of real people's lives and the effect apartheid, and the transition to majority rule, had on them ... An eloquent account of a thoughtful foreign correspondent' – Richard Ellis in the *Sunday Times*